[Handwritten inscription: "Many ... to you on your spiritual journey. Caren Burmeister"]

REMEMBER ME

HOW TO CREATE A SPIRITUAL LEGACY OF LOVE AND LIGHT

BETTY MAY "ALISA" POWELL

CAREN BURMEISTER

COPYRIGHT

It is not death that a man should fear, but he should fear never beginning to live.

– Marcus Aurelius

lain, which only deepened my commitment. I don't believe any single one of these is the only *true* religion. But I have found strength in all of them.

Born the eighth of eleven children, I was delivered by my anxious father and ten-year-old sister at our home in Joplin, Missouri. I've been married four times – twice to the same man – and I have three children. Looking back on it, I can't believe I survived my first husband, Gary's, emotional and physical abuse. He was the father of my children, whom I married when I was sixteen and divorced eight years later.

I'm a totally different person now. Yet, I believe everything happens for a reason.

As I've grown older, I've come to realize that some people think I'm odd. Even at a young age I realized I had psychic abilities. Later, when I asked my mom what I was like as a child, she said I used to predict things were going to happen before they actually did. I've also had spontaneous, mystical experiences of being in another time and space.

I'm not special. I'm not unique. It's just that I'm open to messages as they come to me from Spirit. I've always been sensitive, and I have connected many times with loved ones on the other side. I believe we can all do this if we're receptive, if we work on overcoming our fears, and embrace the mysteries of life.

To me, we're all created in the image of God (Higher Power, Holy One, Spirit, Creator, or Supreme Being). Therefore, I am a co-creator with God. In fact, God's divine spark lives in each of us, a spark that empowers us to heal ourselves and others. God is love, and love is the greatest healer of all.

Along my spiritual journey, I've come to accept that there is no *real* death. When we die, only the ego and the physical body come to an end, not the soul (or subtle consciousness). We let go of the material aspects of life and embody our true essence that is the seat of God.

We may be nothing alike, or maybe we have much in common. Some people don't believe in life after death. That's fine. Some of us believe in reincarnation. That's okay, too. It's all good.

I'm not trying to persuade anyone to adopt my beliefs. Perhaps you're a non-believer, and this spirituality stuff rubs you the wrong way. In that case, take what you need from this book and leave the rest behind.

But I encourage everyone to be open to the divine opportunities that may exist outside our own experience. It can expand our sense of wonder and our depth of love for life. Life is a mystery. When we come to accept that, we begin to forge a path based on faith, not certainty.

On the surface, the world's great religions – Christianity, Judaism, Islam, Buddhism, Hinduism – seem miles apart. But if we dig more deeply, we'll find striking similarities in their positions on the origins of life and the nature of reality. The mystics of these great traditions believe that contemplation, self-reflection, and direct experience prepare us to receive spiritual wisdom.

"We all must find an inner authority that we can trust that is bigger than our own," said Fr. Richard Rohr,[1] a Franciscan priest, teacher, and founder of the Center for Action and Contemplation in Albuquerque, New Mexico.

"If God wants to speak to us, God usually speaks in words that first feel like our own thoughts," Rohr said. "How else could God come to us? We have to be taught how to honor and allow that, how to give it authority, and to recognize that sometimes our thoughts are God's thoughts."

Writing this book is also forcing me to grieve the death of my son, Kevin, and to affirm the significance of the butterfly as a sign of my everlasting love for him.

Recently, while decluttering my office, an old letter from Kevin fell out of my secretary. It's hard to describe the crushing loss I felt re-reading it. Kevin's death nearly ripped my heart and soul apart, and I'd never fully given myself permission to feel it. I just couldn't endure that he had died at thirty-eight years of age. Somehow, I'd just muddled through.

So here I am fifteen years later, feeling Kevin's absence like never before. I remember when we saw the movie, *Annie,* and how people laughed at us afterward, as we sang and danced our way out of the theater. I long to hold him just one more time. I long to call him to hear his voice.

Kevin, I feel you near me now as I sob. All these years I've never allowed myself to feel so much heartache. I carried you in my womb for nine months and now I hold you in my heart forever. Never will I stop loving and missing you, my son.

ANECDOTE

One night I awoke to the sound of my son, Kevin's, voice saying *mom* and *write*. I didn't know what he meant. Was he saying right, as in making something right? Or did he mean write things down. Once I began analyzing it, I was wide awake. So, I heeded the call and started writing. It was the year 2013 and I was starting to tinker with the concept of this book. Looking back on it, I believe Kevin was nudging me to write it.

But there were many setbacks. My husband, Phillip, who had been ill for several years, died in 2015. After that I grew even more certain that I needed to write this book. But where to start? I began to ask the Universe for help. Several months later, I had a heart attack. The surgeon woke me after surgery.

"Mrs. Pearl," he said. "The Lord told me he saved you because you have more work to do."

I knew exactly what that meant: this book.

WHAT IS A SPIRITUAL LEGACY?

"Legacy is every life you touch." — *Oprah*

Our spirituality is the essence of who we are. It's what makes us unique. It's what makes us lovable despite our quirky, annoying flaws. It's the basis of why we do what we do.

These spiritual qualities may be subtle or obvious. Even if we don't recognize them in ourselves, our partners, friends, and family probably do. More than anything, these qualities are reflected in how we treat ourselves and others.

Legacy reaches beyond our life. It honors our basic human wish to be remembered – it offers proof that our life was meaningful. It focuses on what we leave behind to our loved ones and our community. While some legacies include a gift of money or property, that's not the focus of this book.

The legacy we're concerned with is our written story: how we've lived our lives and how the challenges we've overcome have helped shape who we are. We have not grown despite those challenges, but because of them. This includes our character traits, faith in our Higher Power, acts of kindness, and how we have shared our skills and talents.

This book serves two purposes: To help me write my spiritual legacy as I come to terms with my mortality, and to help readers do the same.

The spiritual legacy I'm referring to is an intentional document, a story that passes on our values, character, and how God has shown faithfulness in our life. It will capture who we are, what we've learned about life, how we've evolved, and how we've shared or gifts with others.

It's a personal story promoting the continuity of life, a story that will be precious to our loved ones, their children, and many generations to come.

History shows that our personal stories are universally valued, and welcomed, regardless of our spiritual traditions or life circumstances.

Madeleine L'Engle, a writer whose work reflected her Christian faith and scientific interests, advocated the power of storytelling. As she put it, our personal stories reveal our "faith that the universe has meaning, that our little human lives are not irrelevant, that what we choose to say or do matters, matters cosmically." [1]

As Roshi Joan Halifax prepared for her ordination in the Zen Peacemaker Order, the anthropologist, Buddhist teacher, and counselor to the dying reflected on how death can make us appreciate the "transitory nature of existence." She came to this conclusion while sewing her kesa, an ordination robe made of clothing from people who had died or had been critically ill.

"Why is it we love to listen to our teachers and elders tell a story?" Halifax asked. [2] "Because it's a way that we can find ourselves in a landscape that offers a new and deeper perspective on who we really are. Stories are medicine because they teach us about and prepare us for the experience of change. Through the story, we may connect to a more realistic vision of who we really are."

Patients with advanced illness are often encouraged to tell their story about their spiritual beliefs, values, and experiences while they can. For some, it offers a transformative experience, said Beba Tata, a Mayo Clinic chaplain who was involved with the "Hear My Voice" project in Rochester, Minnesota.

"Through this study I have experienced the power of voice," she said. [3] "Telling their stories was part of the legacy that the people wanted their loved ones to hold on to and remember them by. … I have seen people move from shock to acceptance, from desolation to consolation. I have heard expressions of perseverance, positivity, and hope that have helped people adjust to diagnosis and give comfort during treatment."

OUR ROOTS

There has been a resurgence of interest in our ancestral origins, largely due to the accessibility of at-home DNA testing. As of 2021, the top two testing companies claimed to have 42 million people (combined) in their databases. [4]

But genetic research can only go so far in our search for who we are.

"A connection to our recent ancestors is what compels us to study our genealogy. It is their stories that fascinate us, not their genetic stock," said Nathan H. Lents, a scientist, author, and university professor. [5]

While genetic testing points to our ethnicity, where our ancestors came from, and potential family relationships, a spiritual legacy is much more personal. Offering deep insights into our life, a spiritual legacy will help family and friends come to know us in a way that no biological test ever could. It will help them to understand us and see the meaning and purpose of our lives. Just think: Descendants, many generations down the road, may read it someday.

EXPRESSIONS OF GRIEF AND HEALING

Storytelling is a powerful way to express our grief and keep our loved ones alive. For some, it helps to have an object to hold or touch, like a keepsake or memento to stay connected. It could be as simple as a shell, rock or a pressed flower. Or perhaps a drawing, a piece of clothing or anything that holds special meaning.

For parents who have lost a child, they don't need keepsakes to help them remember their child. They need a tangible and essential connection to sustain them in their grief.

"These objects can serve as lifelines after parents must tear themselves away from their child's body," said Jim Manzardo, [6] a hospital chaplain at Lurie Children's Hospital of Chicago.

Historically, a lock of hair symbolized the depth of one's love for the deceased. In Victorian times, bereaved family members often wore black clothing for a year and kept a lock of their beloved's hair in a jar or a broach. These keepsakes brought comfort, as did other symbolic displays, such as crosses, anchors, or sweet lily-of-the-valley flowers.

To a degree, that practice is still alive today. Known as cremation jewelry or cremation sculpture, these mementos come in glass, metal, or wooden forms infused with the loved one's cremation ashes. They are sold on online stores, as well as urn pendants, or little bottles to hold a lock of hair.

CONTINUITY OF LIFE

I don't think we ever "get over" the death of a loved one. Maybe we're not meant to. After all, I believe the soul is immortal. I believe in the continuity of life – that my loved ones who have died are still present, even though they're physically dead.

As I adapt to their loss, our relationship carries on. Grief experts call this "continuing bonds." I know that my son, grandson, husband, and others who have died are watching over me, guiding me, and communicating with me. In this way, I stay deeply connected to them and gain the benefit of their wisdom.

Our need to remember and to be remembered is universal. The Stanford Center for Integrative Medicine refers this ambition to leave our stamp on the world as "symbolic immortality:"

"In a sense, one escapes death by living afterwards through acts and accomplishments which will be remembered for generations and possibly centuries." [7]

We can achieve symbolic immortality in several ways: Many of us do it by having children. Religious and spiritual people believe their souls are eternal, thus assuring life after death. Others leave an artistic or intellectual legacy through books, films, music, paintings, scientific discoveries, or engineering patents.

I believe that nature, which renews itself in endless life cycles, is also a symbol of immortality. Ecosystems regenerate despite storms, fires, human carelessness, and other catastrophes. Water evaporates and returns to the earth in rain and snow. A dead tree falls to the forest ground, offering worms for woodpeckers, burrows for lizards and squirrels, and a nutritious platform for mushrooms. Its leaves scatter across the forest floor, breaking down into compost that protects moisture in the soil and nourishes other trees.

Why should human consciousness, or the soul, be any different?

ANECDOTE: LUKE MY CANDLE BURNS FOR YOU

A few years ago, Robert and I lit a memorial candle in honor of my grandson, Luke, on the eve of his November 2 birthday. A Jewish tradition, the candle is designed to burn for twenty-six hours. By all rights, it should have gone out the next night, Saturday night. But the candle was still glowing when we left for church Sunday morning. Later that day, I opened a fortune cookie and the message said, "you will soon witness a miracle."

I believe Luke inspired the candle to burn so much longer. I call that a miracle. It was Luke's way of telling me he's alive and well in another time and space. That's why we always need to keep our loved ones who have died in our hearts and minds. These miracles, blessings, and healings surround us – we just have to recognize them.

I like to pray when I'm stressed, grateful, or deeply touched by something. Feel free to pray with me:

Father, Mother, God, angels, teachers, master and guides, and sweet, sweet Holy Spirit: We come to you in prayer, praise, thanksgiving, and gratitude for blessings seen and unseen, known and unknown, and for miracles all around us.
Thank you for the love, light, and healing that's in every one of us. Let that light shine into the world where there may be darkness. Thank you for the joy

*and peace – the peacefulness that always lives
within us.*

*All prayers are delivered in divine timing and divine
order.*

*Thank you, sweet spirit. All is well. And so it is.
Amen.*

PREPARING FOR REFLECTION

At the end of several chapters, there are five questions to encourage contemplation. To prepare, we recommend finding a place, inside or out, where there will be as few distractions as possible. We may also need to release the racing, anxious thoughts in our mind – the judging or analysis that often rents space in our head.

A regular practice of mediation and deep breathing can help us "get out of our head" and focus on what's in our heart, where Gods speaks to us.

There are many free online resources for meditation and deep breathing, including YouTube videos and apps like Insight Timer. Meditation and contemplation can help us experience divine silence so we can hear the "still, small voice within."

This phrase refers to the Bible passage 1 Kings 19:11-13, when God spoke to the prophet Elijah. After he'd won victory over the prophets of the false god, Baal, Elijah learned that Queen Jezebel had issued death threats against him. So he ran for safety to Mount Sinai.

"The Lord sent a mighty wind which broke the rocks in pieces; then He sent an earthquake and a fire, but His voice was in none of them. After all that, the Lord spoke to Elijah in the still small voice, or "gentle whisper." [8]

Rather than use dramatic events, like earthquakes and fires, God spoke to Elijah gently – through divine silence.

QUESTIONS FOR REFLECTION

1. What do you want your family to know about you before you die?

2. Do you have a happy place (real or imagined) where you can find solitude, peace, and renewal?

3. Have you ever felt unconditional love and trust with someone? If so, what did it mean to you?

4. Were you raised in a religious or spiritual home? If so, what impact has that had on your life?

5. If you're a nonbeliever, can you identify with personal evolution in a secular sense?

COMMITTING TO FORGIVENESS

"As I walked out the door toward the gate that would lead to my freedom, I knew if I didn't leave my bitterness and hatred behind, I'd still be in prison." — Nelson Mandela, first Black South African president and 1993 Nobel Peace Prize recipient.

WHEN NELSON MANDELA walked out of prison to his new life of freedom in 1990, he knew he had to forgive his persecutors.

Mandela served twenty-seven years in prison for trying to dismantle government-backed apartheid, or institutionalized racism, in South Africa. He had been sentenced to life in prison for his political activity, including strikes, protests, and sabotage.

He spent most of that time in a cramped, damp concrete cell where he slept on a straw mat and worked daily in a lime quarry.

Once he was released, forgiveness and reconciliation became the heart and soul of Mandela's work: He saw national reconciliation as "the primary task of his presidency."

"He refused to let his enemies control him when he left prison – he forgave them so they wouldn't continue to inhabit his body and control him with continued anger," said former President Bill Clinton in the "Long Walk to Freedom: The Autobiography of Nelson Mandela." [1]

Mandela later founded the Truth and Reconciliation Commission, a court-like restorative justice organization which he felt was crucial for South Africa to become a free democracy. The commission investigated human rights abuses between 1960 and 1994, worked to restore victims' dignity, and created a forgiveness and rehabilitation process for abusers who applied for amnesty.

Mandela didn't wait until the end of his life to offer forgiveness. He's a role model for why we shouldn't either.

Forgiveness frees our spirit and makes us feel much lighter. When we genuinely forgive someone, we release the related toxic feelings of resentment, anger, bitterness, distrust, and revenge. This is why it's important that we do it for ourselves.

As I grew older, I realized I had to forgive everyone I felt had violated my innocence, including my father and my first husband, Gary, the father of my children. I did it for my sake, not theirs.

I like the way Mark D. White, a philosophy professor, puts it:

"Take it from me: holding grudges, or keeping a tally of perceived transgressions, will only weigh you down over time," White said. "It may feel like forgiveness lets the other person 'off the hook' too easily, but think of it as easing your burden instead. It does you no good to keep track of everything everyone else has done to you through the years." [2]

Back in the 1990s, I wrote a letter to my dead father, addressing him as, "Dear son of a bitch."

When I was about eight years old, Dad caught me teasing my younger brother for Dad's awful bowl haircut. I ran, but Dad snatched me up and lopped off my beautiful long, dark hair. I cried and cursed him. After that, no one ever told me I was pretty.

I wrote this letter to him for my own well-being:

"Remember what you did to us? I hate you for the day you cut my hair and for your emotional and physical abuse of us and mom. P.S. Daddy, I love you."

I wrote it so I could live in peace, free of fear and shame.

THE MEMORIES STILL STUNG

Dad wasn't the only person I needed to forgive. During our tumultuous marriage, Gary had apologized dozens of times for his physical and emotional abuse. But I had grown to doubt his sincerity. Eight years and three children later, I divorced him. That was a long time ago.

Despite all those decades, and his death many years ago, the memories still stung. That became apparent when Gary abruptly came to me, telepathically, while my co-author Caren and I were working on the forgiveness chapter of this book.

I knew it was him, but I was stunned by his fierce energy. At the time, I felt vulnerable and caught off guard by his intense remorse and persistence. Maybe that's why he seized the moment. Tears rolled down my cheeks as I pressed out my hand, urging Gary's spirit to stop this imposition. Not now, I told him. I would consider forgiving him, but I needed time.

Until then, I hadn't even considered forgiving Gary. I thought that ugly chapter of my life had been put to bed. But this book is about love and forgiveness. And if I'm not willing to forgive, how can I ask anyone else to do it?

I first met Gary when I was thirteen years old. I was standing in his mother's kitchen when he walked in. As our eyes locked, I heard a voice say, *you're going to marry him.* A few years earlier, my mom had predicted that I would marry a boy with blonde hair and blue eyes, a boy just like Gary.

I know we were meant to be together, and we loved each other. But we were immature and irresponsible – we were just playing house. I was sixteen years old when we married. A year later I gave birth to Kelly, two years after that I delivered Lisa, and in another four years, Kevin.

When Lisa was a newborn, she cried all the time. She was inconsolable. I believe babies sense tension in their home, even though they can't speak.

Early in my pregnancy, I had told myself that I didn't want to have another baby with Gary, who had become an abusive alcoholic just like my Dad. I was afraid that having another baby would make me more dependent on him.

I recalled a time, years later, when Gary followed me up the stairs of our house on a Navy base in California. He had just come home and wanted to know why his friend was there.

"I don't know," I responded. "Why don't you go ask him yourself. He's your friend."

Gary slapped me hard across the face. I ran into the bathroom and threw my wedding rings in the toilet. He stopped me before I flushed the toilet, then dug the rings out.

Now, I was making time to reflect on why Gary had reached out to me and to relive the highs and lows of our marriage. Did we have some good times? Sure. I remember when we sped down the street on his motorcycle singing, *Oh, we ain't got a barrel of money,* a refrain from "Side by Side" performed by Patsy Cline.[3] And there were the joyful times at the births of our three children.

But with the good times came the bad, some very bad. The scariest was when Gary held me hostage for three days in our Portland home, subtly displaying his shotgun to make his intentions known. Our children were quite young then.

Gary wasn't the only one at fault in our marriage. I had messed up, too. In fact, he was angry with me because I had been unfaithful to him. For years, I had borne the brunt of his alcohol-fueled, unwarranted, fits of jealous rage and accusations that I had been with another man. Now, for the first time, he was right: I had slept with the man who would later become my second husband.

Forgiveness goes two ways: one sincerely seeks forgiveness, the other sincerely receives it. I felt those old, painful emotions coming up and realized my soul was asking me to let it go. It would set us both free.

Not wanting to carry the burden any longer, I felt compelled to forgive Gary for all the past abuse, anger, and jealousy. I asked him to forgive me for all the stupid things I had said and done that had hurt him.

I would have missed an opportunity if Gary's spirit hadn't come to me like it did. So, I said a prayer:

> *Believing that you will receive this in spirit, I forgive you Gary for all the hurt and pain of our past together. May you remain in the love and light of God.*

WHILE DECLUTTERING MY OFFICE RECENTLY, I found a handmade birthday card from my daughter, Kelly, and a little clay pot with paper flowers. The card, with its stick drawing of me holding flowers, said:

> *Roses are red*
> *Violets are blue*
> *Mothers are sweet*
> *But are you?*

I can't recall the day she wrote it, nor my reaction. I'm sure her intent was purely innocent – she was only in the second or third grade at the time. How could I be offended? I cried when I read it, touched by her saying, "I hope you have a wonderful day."

Working on this book is bringing up stuff like that.

THE POWER OF LETTING GO

I have to remember that everyone responds to events differently because of our past experience, our karma, and our point of view.

Over the years, I have found great peace by practicing ho'oponopono, a centuries-old Hawaiian practice of reconciliation and forgiveness. A tradition of Indigenous Hawaiian healers, it acknowledges that holding onto resentment only hurts the person who refuses to forgive.

Don't let the tongue twister put you off. Ho'oponopono (ho - opono - pono) is easier to practice than to pronounce. The funny thing is, I didn't even learn about it until after I moved back to the states from Hawaii.

The practice comes from the words ho'o (to make) and pono (right and congruent with ourselves), according to Matt James, Ph.D. By repeating the word pono, it means "doubly right," or being right with ourselves and others.

James is a psychologist who has researched and validated this forgiveness process. He is also a member of the Huna lineage, an ancient Hawaiian system of healing and spiritual development.

"I wanted to verify how it works because ho'oponopono is more than just a concept that I teach. It is a part of my family lineage and how I live my life," James said. [4]

Ho'oponopono can be practiced face-to-face, or silently to yourself without the other person present. It can be just as effective when the work is done internally because we experience everything that happens to us in our minds.

Since we're responsible for our thoughts, we have the power to let go of the resentment and clear the negative connection. But that still doesn't let us off the hook if we need to make things right with someone.

FOUR SIMPLE STEPS

These are the steps and the order isn't that important. This practice has amazing power. You can simply say the words in your head. The power is in your feeling, your intention, and the willingness of the Universe to forgive.

Step 1 - Repentance: I am responsible for the issue and I feel terrible remorse that I caused this.

Step 2 - Forgiveness: With a sincere heart, say please forgive me over and over. Allow ourselves to feel the remorse.

Step 3 - Gratitude: Say thank you to our body for all it does for us. Thank you for being the best we can be. Thank God. Thank the Universe. Thank whoever it was that just forgave us.

Step 4 - Love: Say I love you. Say it to our body, say it to God. Say I love you to the air we breathe, to the house that shelters us. Say I love you to our challenges. Say it over and over. Mean it. Feel it. There is nothing as powerful as love.

ANECDOTE: FORGIVENESS IS WITHIN REACH

Many years ago, my then husband Phillip was in the intensive care unit following a colon operation on New Year's Eve. I was sitting at his bedside when something prompted me to say, "Phillip, you have to apologize to Kelly."

"For what?" he asked.

"You know what. For the way you treated her."

Phillip had raised Kelly from age nine and he hadn't always been kind, patient, or loving with her.

The day after his surgery, Kelly came to visit him. They said hello to each other as she entered the room. His voice cracked and tears welled in his eyes as he called Kelly's name. She approached and took his hand. Feeling a bit awkward, Lisa and I started to leave the room.

"Kelly, I was a bastard," Phillip said. "I'm sorry for the way I treated you."

"I forgave you a long time ago," Kelly said, giving his hand a gentle shake.

QUESTIONS FOR REFLECTION

1. Do you have something for which you feel you need to be forgiven?

2. What's stopping you from going to that person? If they've died, it's not too late.

3. Do you have trouble forgiving yourself?

4. Has someone asked you for forgiveness, but you resisted?

5. Are you still holding a grudge against someone? Is now a good time to let it go?

OUR TRUE ESSENCE IS GOD WITHIN US

"When you look in the mirror, what you see looking back at you – that's God." — Alisa Powell

No one wants to die without their loved ones knowing who they truly were. But the truth is, many of us know little about the life experiences, values, and point of views that shaped our parents, grandparents, and other loved ones. This is why I've written this book.

As I've matured, I've come to appreciate my inborn gifts and spiritual nature. I don't say this to brag, but to acknowledge I have unique God-given abilities, as we all do. We're all pure love and light because we're created in the image and likeness of God.

Some of us are more conscious of this than others. I believe that human nature is an expression of God. To honor God and ourselves, we must love everyone and all of God's creation without condition. It may sound impossible, but it is within reach.

One of my God-given abilities is a strong intuition or knowing, which has at times foreshadowed tragedy. That's what happened on June 11, 2004. I was cleaning Paula's house (house cleaning was my job at the time) and for some reason I'd put my cell phone in my apron pocket instead of leaving it on the counter. One of the TV stations was broadcasting President Ronald Reagan's funeral service. I rarely turned on the television while I worked, but that day I had. Inspiring music played in the background as I began dusting the bedroom. That's when a forceful inner voice told me to, *Sit down, sit down.*

Please let me explain: I often get messages from Spirit this way. So, I wasn't greatly surprised by the voice.

At first, I resisted. I had too much work to do to sit and watch the memorial service. But I finally gave in. As soon as I sat on the bench my entire body quivered. I couldn't explain what was happening at the time. My intuition was setting off alarm bells. Something was terribly wrong, and it was making me quiver all over.

Just then my cell phone rang. I heard the urgent voice of my grandson, Jessie, who was fourteen at the time. He was calling about his brother.

"Grandma, grandma, something's happened to Luke!"

"What, what? Tell me what's wrong?"

"I don't know grandma."

"Jessie, tell me what's happening with Luke. You have to tell me!"

"No grandma, I don't know. I think he's at Shands Hospital. I don't know what's wrong, though.

"I know where Shands is. I'm going there now."

"No grandma, come to the house," he said calmly, considering the circumstances.

Why did I have my cellphone on me that day? Only God knew. I called Paula and told her something terrible had happened. I apologized profusely for having to leave her house a mess.

As I drove to Luke's house, I repeatedly screamed, "Let it not be true. Let it not be true. God help me. Help me! Give me strength and courage. I need strength and courage. Not for me, but for them. For everyone else. I need it for them!"

When I parked the car and stepped out, an officer walked over. "Are you the grandmother?" "Yes, I'm the grandma. Is he

…?" My knees buckled. I nearly went down but caught myself and stood up. I'd asked for strength and courage, and I got it.

The officer turned to me tenderly. "He's OK now."

Initially I didn't understand. But on a soul level I did. Luke was dead. How did I know? I just knew it in my gut.

Even before I got to the house, I knew he was dead. I knew he was gone. This officer had just confirmed it. I called Paula back. "Luke is dead, my grandson is dead. I'm sorry I didn't finish cleaning your house."

Paula said she was sorry and insisted that I not worry about it: "Just go and take care of your family."

When I walked into the house, my daughter, Kelly, Luke's mother, was sitting at the kitchen table. She turned to me.

"Mom, he's gone …"

"I know. I know."

Then she told me what had happened. Luke, who was sixteen years old, had hung himself from a tree in the backyard.

Suddenly I knew. The moment Luke's soul ascended I had felt it. Just as he was moving out of his body, something was moving out of mine. I knew the moment he took his last breath. Why? Because we had a loving, soul-to-spirit connection to the source I call God.

My meditation on the indwelling presence of God was included in "Intuitive Intelligence: Welcoming the Guest," [1] a book written by my friend, Elisabeth Mandt:

Your soul, your spirit is crying for God.
But God lives within you.
He is not in any teachings,
Not in the churches, not in the synagogues.
The answer is within you.
God is deep within the chambers of your heart.

LOVE AND LIGHT

The message that there is only love and light came to me years ago at a spiritual retreat in Arizona. While meditating, I was overcome by a brilliant light that triggered the memory of my mother, who had died a few years earlier.

"Where is my mother?" I asked God. That's when I heard the words, *there's only love and light*. It struck me to the core, and I wept without shame. From that moment on, I've never had a fear of death or dying. I accepted that Mom wasn't dead, she had just taken another form.

I was standing next to Mom when she took her last breath on Dec. 7, 1987. When I entered her hospital room, I walked over and whispered in her ear: "Hi Mom, it's Betty. I love you. Are you ready to go back to Jesus?"

She didn't respond. In a coma, surrounded by her children and grandchildren, I knew she wasn't afraid. Mom had told me years earlier that she'd had two near-death experiences. Like many others who've experienced their soul releasing from their body and entering the afterlife, it had a profound effect on her. She no longer feared death.

Mom had in fact been declared clinically dead and described both experiences as glorious. The first time, she was at home in her sick bed. She said she recalled floating above her body looking down at the doctor and her mother, who was sobbing. She saw and heard everything that occurred in the room. Then she slipped back into her physical body and recovered from her illness.

In her second near-death experience, Mom spent considerably more time outside her body. She described a luminous scene of a river bordered by flowering trees and shrubs where Jesus appeared as a beautiful, brilliant, blinding light.

Now, for the third and final time, Mom was following that warm light to eternal peace. When she exhaled for the last time on this earth, her next "inhalation" was on the other side.

LISTEN TO THE HEART

We don't "get over" the death of a loved one – we get through it, moment by moment, hour by hour, and day by day. So many years have passed since Kevin's death: I thought I had gone through all the stages of grief, many times over.

But grief is a funny thing. Eventually, we start getting on with our daily life and the things that distract us from our anguish. Then we shift to thinking about how much we miss our loved one, or we look at old photos or recall certain memories that take us back to tears.

It wasn't until I was deep into this book that I realized I hadn't allowed myself to feel the gut-wrenching emotional pain that comes with losing a child. I hadn't made time to listen to my heart. The still, small voice within me.

Writing this book is forcing me to do just that.

In difficult times like this, meditation teacher Llewellyn Vaughan-Lee encourages us to "look inward to the deeper roots of our being where our soul nourishes us." [2]

"We know how to struggle and fight, but not how to be silent and receptive. We have forgotten how to look and listen," said Vaughan-Lee, who practices Sufism, the mystical branch of Islam that emphasizes introspection and spiritual closeness with God.

God instructs us to be fully present in the moment, to reconnect with what's deepest within us and sacred around us. He urges us to harmonize with nature and renew our energy through meditation and reflection.

When we're ready, of course. As they say, when the student is ready, the teacher will appear.

There came a time, when Kevin was sick, that I began to record our phone conversations so I could listen to them later, after he died. He always opened with, "High guys. What's happening? I was just thinking about you and thought I'd give you a call."

In his late thirties, Kevin found a lump under his arm. The doctor didn't have good news.

Toward the end of Kevin's life, I went to visit him at his home in Key West. One day he was tending the garden in his backyard, which he simply adored. I stood back and watched in silence. I watched him working in his garden because I knew I'd never see anything like it again. He walked up the steps to greet me and we sat on a bench. "Kevin, hold me," I pleaded. "Hold me."

He took me in his arms and held me like a mother holds a child. He held me like he was the parent. It was so tender and sweet. We knew he was dying. I'll never forget that bittersweet moment. That embrace. We just sat there. No words were spoken. It was one of the last times I saw him. I think of it often.

Phillip and I had gone with Kevin to the doctor. His treatments weren't working. He didn't live a year past his diagnoses. Kevin was only thirty-eight years old when he died on June 24, 2004 – thirteen days after Luke.

Back in the 1990s, Kevin had told me that he was gay. At the time, AIDS was the number one cause of death of young men in the U.S. Eventually, Kevin developed AIDS-related cancer. After he died, these words came to me:

> *Who would love me if not you, Mom?*
> *Who would love me if not you, Dad?*
> *Who would love me if not you, Sister?*
> *Who would love me if not you, Brother?*
> *God loves me ... I am His precious child.*

ANECDOTE: THE FLUTTER OF WINGS

Butterflies are the hallmark of my spiritual journey. They represent my deep connection to Kevin, symbolizing metamorphosis and our deep love for one another.

Perhaps more than any other creature on earth, the butterfly is the embodiment of spiritual growth and transcendence. Across many traditions and religions, its journey from cater-

pillar to chrysalis to butterfly is a symbol of new begin-
nings, personal growth, hope, and resurrection.

Just think of it: This elusive creature abandons everything it has
known to embrace an entirely new way of being. Most of us can
only dream of achieving such a remarkable transformation.

As it flitters about, its delicate wings, covered in thousands
of tiny scales that shimmer in extraordinary colors and
patterns, flap in a figure-eight motion, enticing children to
chase it with abandon.

Each year, millions of monarch butterflies use celestial navi-
gation and the sun to make their 3,000-mile-trek from
Canada to Mexico. With a brain no larger than the head of a
pin, "They hold a treasure-trove of navigational mechanisms that keep screaming out to be understood," an
admiring scientist said in a 2010 study. [3]

During my visit to Key West, Kevin showed me a caterpillar
on his patio. He gently raised a leaf with the creature
perched on it and placed it in a jar. He fed it and kept it out
of direct sunlight, eager to nurture it and witness its metamorphosis. But it wasn't meant to be.

Kevin knew he was dying. He didn't know when, but like
the caterpillar he was about to go through major changes. In
his own way, he knew he was on a journey to become something else.

Since Kevin's death, butterflies have always reminded me that his spirit is near. I bought a skirt adorned with butterflies. I told my friends about my butterfly connection to Kevin and how they often seem to appear out of nowhere. On my next birthday, every card, wrapping paper, and gift was adorned with butterflies.

Once, I bought a butterfly plant from a vendor near my home. A huge butterfly caught my attention and I spoke to it: "Hi Kevin. I love you. I miss you." (I always talk to butterflies.) I drove the plant home and when I got out of the car the same butterfly flew right to me.

Butterflies also made an appearance on Christmas 2019, when my husband, Robert, and I joined his family for dinner and a gift exchange. With anticipation, I tore into the big present placed at my feet. As the crisp wrapping paper fell to the floor, I saw the butterflies on the wooden plaque and started to cry. The room fell silent. Beneath the image appeared this inspirational message:

> *Whisper*
> *I love you*
> *to a butterfly*
> *it will fly to heaven*
> *to deliver your message.*

Gentle tears gave way to deep, racking sobs. Their gift acknowledged how much I have missed my son and that I will always have an abiding connection to him.

The following night, before I went to sleep, I asked Kevin to send me a butterfly the next day. Sure enough, a butterfly appeared outside the window while I ate breakfast. Then it was joined by another. Once again, Kevin confirmed he got the message. Just as I expected.

QUESTIONS FOR REFLECTION

1. Do you have a favorite insect, animal, or plant that's a metaphor for your life, or someone you lost?

2. Have you ever been told to get over it? If so, what was your reaction?

3. Do you have trouble being silent and receptive? What's standing in your way?

4. How do you make time to listen to your heart?

5. Do you believe we are created in the image and likeness of God? That human nature is an expression of God?

LOVE NEVER DIES

"Love is patient, love is kind. It does not envy, it does not boast, it is not proud. It does not dishonor others, it is not self-seeking, it is not easily angered, it keeps no record of wrongs. Love does not delight in evil but rejoices with the truth. It always protects, always trusts, always hopes, always perseveres. Love never fails." — 1 Corinthians 13:4-8 New International Version

WHEN A PERSON DIES, it doesn't mean our love for them dies, too. While the physical body eventually meets its end, I believe our spirit is eternal.

Healthy grief comes from building a new and different relationship with our deceased loved one, says counselor Litsa Williams, the co-founder of the website What's Your Grief?

Several years ago, Williams praised the book, "Continuing Bonds: New Understandings of Grief."

Written for psychologists and grief counselors, it challenges modern styles of grief that promote closure, acceptance, and moving on.

Continuing bonds takes a different approach to grief. Under this process, grief is ongoing. It becomes a permanent part of us. We stay connected to our loved one the rest of our life because doing so helps us cope with the loss. Best of all, it confirms we're not crazy!

"Its ideas were both obvious and revolutionary, all at once," Williams said.[1] "The bad news? Most regular people haven't gotten the memo yet. The old school models of detachment and letting go still run deep in our pop culture and our societal expectations."

For years, I've had continuing bonds with my deceased loved ones without even knowing it. I perform rituals, such as burning candles, to honor them. I seek their advice when I have to make tough decisions. I've asked them to intercede on my behalf for divine intervention. I speak to butterflies that symbolize Kevin.

How I stay connected is an expression of my love for them. It means being vulnerable and open to mystery and uncertainty. It means learning the signs they use to contact me. It means I make time for contemplation, to be aware of my surroundings, and to pay attention to my dreams.

Spirits commonly use dreams to speak to us. Just days after my friend's grandson was struck and killed by a car, he told me he had a deeply touching dream. He adored his grandson, who had been born without a left arm. The young man, who was not yet twenty, never let that stop him from surfing, traveling, and living life to its fullest. In the dream, the grandson appeared in bodily form, inviting his grandfather to take a close look at him.

"Look at me granddaddy. Now I have both arms. But you loved me when I only had one."

We never know when a loved one might reach out to us. In this case, the grandson appeared within days of his death to let his grandfather know that, now in God's hands, he had become whole.

There are many ways we can stay connected with our deceased loved ones. Here are some examples:

- Having conversations with them
- Visiting places where we feel close to them
- Visitation dreams
- Food cravings
- Sensing their presence
- Feeling a reassuring touch
- Smelling their fragrance

- Weird electrical activity or items inexplicably falling off a shelf
- The appearance of meaningful words or phrases they shared during their life
- Hearing their voice, perhaps calling your name
- Music
- Intuitive knowing
- Verbal or non-verbal messages during prayer or deep meditation

Sometimes, loved ones reach out to protect us, like Kevin did last year. I was finally throwing away his journals and pictures when a picture of a green-eyed, black-and-white kitten caught my eye. I got a clear message to retrieve the cat picture from the trash can. I've learned to listen to that inner voice, even if it doesn't make sense.

The next morning the same kitten appeared in my dream. Sitting outside on the patio facing the sliding glass doors, the cat motioned to a tear in the screen where it had separated from the door frame. The cat in my dream told me to fix it or else my beloved Samantha – an indoor cat with no claws – would get out. Then the kitten flew off as if it had wings.

I told Phillip about the dream. He examined the screen door, found the tear that we had never noticed, and fixed it. The hole was right where Samantha used to stretch out on the floor. Left unchecked, Samantha surely would have found the opening and snuck out.

That's how Kevin relates to me. People on the other side know things we don't know. This time, Kevin sent me a message through a green-eyed kitten.

LEARNING TO LOVE AGAIN

During our forty years together, I'd always thought Phillip was my true love (we had married, divorced, and married again). When he was ill and near the end of his life, Phillip teased me, predicting I'd get together with someone else after he died. No, I told him, I'll will never be with another man.

So, when I started to feel love again I was taken by surprise. It began at a church party. My friends nearly had to drag me there since Phillip had died only three months before. I was chatting with someone when I saw a friend across the court-yard struggling to seat her husband, who had a crippling disorder. I ran to help and so did Robert, coming from the other side of the courtyard.

Once the man was safely seated, Robert put his arms around our shoulders and said, "two of my favorite ladies." In the awkward silence, I noticed the peace sign on a chain around Robert's neck. I recalled that we used to sing together in the church choir.

"Let's have salad," Robert said, asking me out on a lunch date.

"I thought you'd never ask," I responded.

I don't know where that response came from. As I turned my head, I saw Robert's youngest daughter in the background cheering for her father. Apparently, she had overheard the conversation and approved.

Later, I was struck by a pang of guilt. Was it too soon to be feeling giddy like this? I'd never experienced such a jumble of emotions. My stomach was in knots, but my heart was jumping for joy. I felt like I was sixteen again. This was crazy. What would people think?

When I got home, I looked in a mirror and laughed out loud. "Phillip, I'm going on a date."

The next morning at church Robert asked me to sit with him. When the service ended, he invited me to lunch with him and his daughters. We continued our conversation at his house, where we talked for hours about his deceased wife, my deceased husband, his kids, and my kids.

When we said goodbye, butterflies swirled in my stomach. We've been together ever since.

Feeling awkward about the situation, I went to see my friend, Rabbi Robert Goodman. I told him I'd met someone special, and that we were seeing each other.

"Oh Alisa, I'm so happy for you," Goodman said.

"But Rabbi, Phillip just died."

"Life is for the living," he said with a comforting expression. "Phillip would want that."

The rabbi had been in the same position himself, having remarried more than a year after his first wife died. So, in his own way, Phillip was giving me permission to live and love again.

This is why I believe love never dies. I still loved Phillip. I still loved his true essence. But I believe we can love more than one person at a time.

GIVING YOUR PARTNER PERMISSION

Now, I'm going to suggest what may seem like an impossible conversation. That is, giving our spouse or partner permission to find love again if we die before they do.

That's exactly what children's author Amy Krouse Rosenthal did when she announced to the world, in a 2017 column in The New York Times, that she was dying of cancer and wanted her husband to remarry. Written like a dating profile, her column was published ten days before she died of ovarian cancer.

"I have been married to the most extraordinary man for 26 years," she stated in her column, "You May Want to Marry

My Husband." I was planning on at least another 26 together." [2]

But life had other plans. She praised her husband, Jason, touting his pleasant nature, good looks, sharp dressing, and flair for cooking. Amy's column went viral, attracting more than five million readers. And, as of late 2021, Jason was seeing someone.

In his essay, published in the same newspaper a year after Amy died, Jason thanked her for giving him "permission to make the most out of my remaining time on this planet." [3]

"Talk with your mate, your children and other loved ones about what you want for them when you are gone," Jason said in his column. "By doing this, you give them liberty to live a full life and eventually find meaning again. There will be so much pain, and they will think of you daily. But they will carry on and make a new future, knowing you gave them permission and even encouragement to do so."

We don't need to publish our permission. But I highly recommend having this conversation before it's too late. It may feel like a daunting task, but it's just too important to neglect. Why not bring it up during a discussion on end-of-life care wishes and plans? That might be a good time to start the conversation.

Some months ago, I told Robert that I want him to find a companion after I die. He instantly responded, "You don't have to worry about that because I'm going to go first."

"No, I am," I said, half-jokingly.

It's still uncomfortable to talk about it. I think that's why we dodge the issue.

I brought it up again, whispering the message to him as we were falling asleep. I keep reassuring Robert and he keeps telling me I don't need to worry about it.

I don't want Robert to be alone and I know he doesn't want to be alone, either. Plenty of studies have shown that widowhood causes loneliness and isn't good for our physical and mental health, particularly for men. Maybe for that reason, widowers tend to remarry more often than widows. About 18 percent of widowed men remarry and 7 percent live with a partner, whereas just 4 percent of widowed women get married again and 3 percent cohabit with a partner. [4]

ANECDOTE: HIS LOVE IS STILL ALIVE

The week after Phillip died, I heard him call me by name from the kitchen.

"Yes, honey," I replied, startled. It didn't take long for me to doubt what I'd heard.

Several nights later, I felt Phillip touch my back. I was nearly asleep, yet I could feel the warmth and weight of his hand on my skin. It felt so real I thought he was still in bed with me. It was the touch that had always made me feel safe, like he'd always done to say goodnight.

A few nights later, I was awoken by a big thud in the living room. Alarmed, my cat jumped off my bed. I thought someone had broken into the house. Terrified, I jumped up and turned on the lights. But the doors were still locked, and nothing had fallen to the floor. I don't think I slept a wink for days after that.

I knew without a doubt it was Phillip. It was the same sound he'd made when he'd fallen so many times before his final trip to the hospital.

Even though Phillip died, he was still in my heart. His love was still alive. We were still connected. Spirit comes to us in many forms. Energy doesn't die, it just changes form. Death is nothing more than a fresh new beginning in another time and space.

QUESTIONS FOR REFLECTION

1. Do you perform rituals to honor a loved one who has died?

2. Have you ever connected to a deceased loved one by sensing their presence, a powerful dream, an electrical anomaly, or intuitive knowing?

3. Would you want your spouse to remarry, or find love again, after you die?

4. Have you had the difficult conversation with your significant other about finding love again if you die before they do?

5. Has your significant other given you permission to love again?

GRIEF IS UNIVERSAL

"As we come forth, so we shall return." — Ecclesiastes 5:14

HUMANS DO IT. Neanderthals did it. Even animals do it. It seems that all of us grieve.

There's archeological proof that Neanderthals, our "evolutionary cousins" who lived in Europe and Asia, intentionally buried their dead starting around 100,000 years ago.

Animals respond to death in their own way. In 2010, a wildlife biologist watched a Rothschild's giraffe stand vigil by her dead calf in Kenya for three days without eating or drinking, according to the National Wildlife Federation.[1] Four decades earlier in Tanzania, Jane Goodall witnessed a young chimpanzee stop eating and grow gaunt and lethargic after its mother died. The young chimp died a month later.

Now, we can't prove those animals actually felt grief. But there are numerous eye-witness accounts and studies with unmistakable evidence that animals experience deep feelings.

Grief is universal. But even amongst us humans, no one experiences it the same way.

"There is not a typical response to loss as there is no typical loss," said grief expert David Kessler, who co-authored the bestseller, "Life Lessons," with Elisabeth Kübler-Ross, a psychiatrist and hospice pioneer. [2]

Kübler-Ross was known for developing the five-stages of grief: denial, anger, bargaining, depression, and acceptance. This theory became widely popular after her ground-breaking book, "On Death and Dying," was published in 1969.

Her grief cycle resonates with mourners who seek a sense of order, validation, and hope as they experience over-whelming grief. But her theory was actually meant for patients who'd been diagnosed with a terminal illness, not people grieving the loss of a loved one. It was never intended to forecast a linear progression because these stages could overlap, occur together, or never occur at all.

In his latest book, "Finding Meaning: The Sixth Stage of Grief," Kessler shows how we can move beyond acceptance to find meaning by honoring the loss of the unique and valued loved one.[3] Kessler speaks from personal experience: his book was published three years after his twenty-one-year-old son died of an accidental drug overdose.

MANY TRADITIONS

Rituals are also universal, in religious and secular life, because they mark fundamental rites of passage, provide meaning to our experience, and help us connect with one another.

A nation built by immigrants seeking freedom of expression and religion, the United States is home to people of many faiths and cultures. According to a 2019 Pew Research Center survey, about 65 percent of U.S. adults considered themselves Christians, and 26 percent identified themselves "religiously unaffiliated" (atheist, agnostic, or no religion).[4] Judaism is the second-largest religion, practiced by 2 percent of the population, followed by Islam, Buddhism, and Hinduism.

When it comes to death, each religion has its own customs. For example, some religions prohibit cremation, viewing it as sacrilegious. Others believe cremation is sacred – that it releases the person's spirit from the physical body so it can be reborn.

While Christians once believed cremation interfered with the physical resurrection of the body, many have grown to accept it, in large part because land is scarce in crowded cities.

"Over the past four years, cremations have surpassed burials as the most popular end-of-life option in the United States," according to the National Funeral Directors Association.[5] "By 2040, the cremation rate in the U.S. is projected to be 78.7%."

Now, there are many creative options available after cremation: We can memorialize our loved ones by having their ashes pressed into a vinyl record, glass art, jewelry, or even a biodegradable urn that helps their ashes grow into a tree.

Attending a funeral or memorial service is one of the most time-honored ways to show respect to a friend or family member who has died. This invites mourners to face the emotional pain of their loss and to express their thoughts and feelings.

While some people may be uncomfortable with the heightened emotions or unique customs, the show of support can mean the world to devastated family and friends.

Attendance can feel intimidating if the deceased practiced a different faith than our own. To put people at ease, we've summarized the etiquette and funeral customs of the five major religions. Please note that these rituals vary widely based on various sects and evolving religious and cultural traditions.

CHRISTIAN SERVICE

Christian services tend to reflect the personal wishes of the deceased, and his or her family, and their particular faith. Traditions range from elaborate formal wakes and funerals to simple – sometimes even joyful – memorial services to honor and celebrate the loved one's life. Services usually occur within three days to a week after death. However, memorial services can take place several months later.

A funeral service, where the deceased's body is present, is the most formal. Taking place at a church or funeral home, the casket may remain open or closed for the service. Some Christians hold a wake (or viewing) before the service so loved ones may offer their final goodbyes and have time to socialize.

Funerals follow an order, often outlined in a handout to guests. This includes hymns, Bible readings, and prayers to glorify God and ask Him to grant the deceased eternal peace in heaven. Toward the end of the funeral, family and close friends give eulogies, sharing personal stories that honor the loved one's life and comfort the bereaved. Funerals usually conclude by driving the body to a nearby cemetery, where there may be a brief graveside service.

For less formal ceremonies, family and friends may organize a memorial service, or celebration of life service, after the body has been buried or cremated. Still dignified and respectful, this service tends to make room for more expressions of joy – perhaps even laughter. Often, following a funeral or memorial service, the family will host a reception with food at the church or a family member's home.

Etiquette

Funeral attire is formal, and mourners usually dress in black or dark colors. That means a full suit for men, or at least dress pants with a button-up shirt and tie. Women often wear a conservative black or dark-colored dress. Usually, the first two rows of seating at the service are reserved for immediate family.

Flowers, a symbol of new life, are a nice way to express love for the person who died and to comfort grieving family members, but they aren't mandatory. They may be sent to the funeral home or to the family's home. Cards and sympathy gifts, like food, plants, or money, should be given to the family as discreetly as possible.

JEWISH SERVICE

Under Jewish customs, the burial should take place as quickly as possible following the death, traditionally within twenty-four hours. But for practical reasons, burials are often postponed a few days so family members may attend the ceremonies.

Jewish funerals may take place at a cemetery, funeral parlor, or a synagogue. They tend to be a simple, somber affair to comfort mourners and commemorate the loved one's life. Mourners will recite prayers, such as the Prayer of Mercy and the Mourner's Kaddish, and offer eulogies to honor the deceased and comfort the living. The body, which has been cleansed and dressed in a plain white shroud before the service, is not displayed during the funeral.

While cremation has traditionally been discouraged in the Jewish tradition, it's not as taboo as it once was, and some Reform Jews (less orthodox) are now choosing cremation.

If the funeral occurs somewhere other than the burial site, mourners will follow the body to the cemetery. They carry the casket, or follow it, from the hearse to the grave, making seven pauses along the way to consider how they've lived their own lives.

Once the casket is set in the ground, mourners cover it with a shovelful of dirt then place the shovel back in the ground to avoid passing personal grief from one person to the next.

Sitting shiva for seven days after the burial is a sacred part of the Jewish funeral tradition. Family members often burn a candle and cover mirrors to focus attention on the deceased. They may wear a torn black ribbon on their clothes to represent the tear in their hearts.

Etiquette

Modesty is important. Men typically wear long pants and a dress shirt while women wear dresses or skirts that fall below the ankle.

Flowers or money are not traditionally offered during the funeral or shiva. It is not customary to place flowers on the grave.

However, gifts of food that are easy to serve, such as fruit baskets or food trays, are appreciated during shiva because family members are supposed to avoid activities like cooking during this time. While shiva is a solemn period for spiritual healing, it's also time for family and friends to remember the deceased, recall stories that honor them, and pray that their soul finds proper rest.

ISLAMIC SERVICE

Muslims attend funerals within a day of their loved one's death, or as soon as possible thereafter, to join the last rites and prayers for the deceased's safe release to the afterlife. The body, which has been bathed and covered in plain cloth by family members or the spouse, is present but shrouded.

In a simple ceremony led by an Imam (priest in the Muslim community), the mourners form at least three lines, with men in the front and women and children behind them. Turning to face the Islamic holy city of Mecca, they recite the Salat al-Janazah, a funeral prayer seeking forgiveness for the deceased and for all Muslims.

Immediately after the funeral, the body is taken to the cemetery to be buried facing Mecca. Muslims do not believe in cremation (or autopsies).

Traditionally, there is a three-day mourning period when the family receives visitors and condolences, usually in the family home. A meal is often served, and guests may be asked to stay and socialize the entire day. Gifts of food, such as a dried fruit and nut basket, baked goods, or meals that can be reheated, are welcomed as it's considered inappropriate for the family to cook during this time of grief. Any food offerings should be halal out of respect for Islamic dietary restrictions.

Etiquette

In general, outwardly lavish displays are discouraged. Men and women should dress modestly, avoiding tight or revealing clothes to attend an Islamic funeral. Women usually wear a head scarf. Shoes must be removed before entering the prayer hall of a mosque.

Muslims prefer not to bring gifts, flowers, or donations to a Muslim funeral or burial. Personal visits, sympathy cards, or handwritten notes about the good deeds and attributes of the deceased are considered a nice way to share grief. Donations may be made in the name of the deceased to religious projects, charitable organizations, or individuals in need.

HINDU SERVICE

The three-part Hindu death ritual starts with an open-casket funeral, or wake, for loved ones and well-wishers within one to two days of a death. By this time, the body has been cleansed and dressed in simple clothes and marked with sacred ash across the forehead. The body may be adorned with flowers and sandalwood. By custom, there is no touching of the body during the wake.

The funeral service may take place at a funeral home or a family member's home. Hindus at the service will participate in chants and mantras, and last rites will be performed by a Hindu priest or the oldest male family member. Loved ones, friends, and neighbors are welcomed as a support system for the family.

Afterward, the body is taken to the crematorium for the second stage – the cremation, which is considered a private matter for close family. Burials (and embalming) are uncommon in the Hindu tradition.

Cremation is revered in Hindu custom, as they believe it helps the soul escape the body and live on through reincarnation. The cremation may be followed the next day by an immersion ceremony, when the family releases the loved one's ashes into a river or the ocean. Hindus believe all water sources are sacred.

The third part of the Hindu funeral custom is the shraddha, a period of mourning which takes place about ten days after the loved one's death. Family of the deceased are prohibited from attending places of worship because they are believed to be spiritually impure during this time.

Etiquette

Hindus don't wear black to funerals as they consider it inappropriate. Instead, guests should wear white and dress conservatively, with women covering their arms and knees. If the funeral takes place at a Hindu temple, it is appropriate to wear sandals, as everyone will remove their shoes before entering the temple to pray.

Guests are not expected to bring food to a Hindu wake, but flowers are welcomed. Guests who are invited to the immersion ceremony may bring fruit.

BUDDHIST SERVICE

Buddhist funerals are marked by peace and serenity, focusing on impermanence and mortality that brings the deceased's soul closer to Nirvana. Death is not seen as an end, but as a transition from one form to another. Still, it is acceptable for mourners to show grief and acknowledge the loss of the loved one.

The funeral usually occurs within a week after death, often at a funeral home rather than a temple. An altar is set up to display the deceased's portrait and an image of the Buddha, along with offerings of candles, incense, flowers, and fruit.

Typically, a monk delivers a sermon and performs rites, such as pouring water from a vessel into an overflowing cup. They may also lead chanting and sutras (prayers), encouraging mourners to contemplate the transient nature of life and to perform good deeds on the deceased person's behalf. If a monk is not available, someone else may conduct the service.

Mourners are expected to approach the open casket to say goodbye to the loved one and to bow toward them as a sign of respect and appreciation.

After the ceremony, the casket may be buried in a cemetery, but cremation is more common in the Buddhist tradition.

. . .

Etiquette

Family members wear white, often with a headband or armband, and may walk with a stick to symbolize that grief has left them needing support. They may also burn incense and ring gongs or bells. While white is the color of grieving for the family, friends often wear black.

For a temple ceremony, men should wear a tie and women a dress or skirt and blouse. Mourners must remove their shoes before entering the temple and clothing should be suitable for sitting on the floor during meditation. No head covering is required.

Flowers or donations may be sent to the family, but gifts of food are considered inappropriate. Guests may also make a donation to a designated charity in the name of the loved one.

ANECDOTE: BATHING LUKE

By tradition, Jews practice a cleansing ritual, known as tahara, to prepare the body of the deceased for burial. Traditionally, the ritual is performed by specially trained Jews who follow strict procedures as they recite prayers and psalms.

After Luke's death, it was all we could do just to get the coroner to release his body. Luke's mother, Kelly, and I hadn't been able to see him because of the autopsy, which Florida law requires to confirm the cause of death if suicide is suspected.

Finally, Luke's body was released and the funeral home gave us permission to use one of its private rooms. Finding Luke's body dressed in a hospital gown, we prepared his soul for its journey back home to God. I felt this act of intimacy was important. Otherwise, we would never have had our final moments with Luke.

Kelly prayed over Luke while I lovingly bathed him with a wet cloth, starting with his face and his hands. I could see the long autopsy scar on his chest and abdomen. When I got to his feet, I cradled them in my hands and kissed them. Then I said I love you and we left the room. Days later, Luke was cremated.

Since ancient times, families have bathed the dead as an act of purification and to show affection for their loved one. I think this helped us accept that Luke wasn't in his body anymore. He was free. He had gone home to God.

QUESTIONS FOR REFLECTION

1. Can you relate to the five stages of grief: denial, anger, bargaining, depression, and acceptance? Has it helped you understand the grieving process?

2. Do you want friends and family to remember you in a funeral or a memorial service?

3. Do you want your service to be somber, or more light-hearted? What would that service look like?

4. Have you attended a service that was especially comforting and uplifting? What might you want to borrow from that experience for your own service?

5. Do you want to see your loved one's body to say goodbye and find closure?

FEAR OF DEATH AND HOW TO TALK ABOUT IT

"We have to create the right space for people to be less frightened. If you go into yourself deeply enough, truth is there. Life and death are one." — *Peggy Hitchcock, Walking Each Other Home*

HAS anyone ever considered how many ways we avoid saying someone has died? I chuckled out loud when I recently stopped to think about it.

It's only human nature to avoid unpleasant topics. In Western culture, death certainly tops the list. In wartime, we use the term "casualties" to refer to soldiers who have been killed or maimed, and "collateral damage" for innocent civilians who have died or been injured in war.

It seems we'll do most anything to avoid saying Joe, Susan, or Barbara has died. It's almost comical when you think about it.

But there may be circumstances when we want a gentler way to tell someone their loved one has died. That's why our language offers expressions to soften the impact. That includes euphemisms (like the military uses above) and metaphors, like having a "broken heart."

"Being heartbroken or having a broken heart is metaphorical language to describe the sensation in one's chest of intense grief," according to "Languages of Grief: A Model for Understanding the Expressions of the Bereaved."[1]

Let's face it, talking about death is just plain awkward. No wonder people stay silent: it's sure better than saying something we'll regret later. Take my car salesman for example. Having no idea that Phillip had died several weeks after we bought a car from him, the salesman called to see what we thought of the new vehicle. When I filled him in, he said he was sorry to hear that Phillip had died. Several moments of awkward silence passed.

"Well, he's in a better place," the salesman said.

"How do you know that?" I asked.

"Well, living with you, I know he's in a better place."

I laughed: I knew he meant it as a joke. I told him that love never dies and there's really no such thing as death, at least not for the soul. The salesman apologized for his flippant remark and begged my forgiveness. I accepted and let him off the hook.

It just shows how tongue-tied we can get when talking about death. There's no shortage of creative ways to tiptoe around it.

KICKED THE BUCKET?

Some people will go to great lengths to avoid saying that someone died. This list shows real effort and ingenuity. In some cases, the origins of these euphemisms date back hundreds of years:

- Bit the dust
- Croaked
- Grim reaper
- Kicked the bucket
- Dearly departed
- Went to heaven
- Lost her battle
- Went home to Jesus
- Gone
- Gone to meet her maker
- Gone to a better place
- Back to source
- Gone back home
- Took her last breath
- At peace
- In a better place
- Went to the great beyond
- She is now singing with the angels
- Went to be with the Lord
- Passed away
- Lost her life

- Made the transition
- Six feet under
- Belly up
- Dead as a doornail
- Checked out
- Bought the farm
- Not with us anymore

FOR ME, the butterfly is a metaphor for my son, Kevin. For someone else, it might be an old gravestone worn by wind, salt, and storms in an English seaside cemetery.

"These gravestones have become works of art, a metaphor for grief itself – the elements of which are expressed in various combinations and may be transformed over time. Given the lack of inscription, the reader is free to interpret the gravestone's meaning." [2]

It takes a real change of heart to begin to view death as a part of life, said Ram Dass, a psychologist and spiritual teacher who promoted conscious aging and dying. In our culture, we treat death as something unnatural, he said. We don't embrace it. We're too afraid to die.

Ram Dass has shared many profound statements about death. One of the best came from his conversation with a spirit guide, Emmanuel, who spoke him telepathically through a medium:

> "Emmanuel, I often deal with the fear of death in this culture. What should I tell people about dying?
>
> Tell them it's absolutely safe! It's like taking off a tight shoe." [3]

Ram Dass' fear of death faded after spending several years in India between 1967 and 1972. In his last book, "Walking Each Other Home: Conversations on Loving and Dying," he spoke of seeing bodies of the dead wrapped in a sheet, placed in a rickshaw and taken to a place where bodies were burned in public while the community chanted the name of God.

"Everybody, including children, would stop and notice," Ram Dass said. "Death was right out in the open, a natural part of life. It wasn't an error or a failure. It was part of life." [4]

HOW TO OFFER SUPPORT

I think we're afraid to say someone died because it triggers fear. It sounds so final. But that says more about our personal beliefs than it does our choice of words.

We all want to support our friends and family during a difficult time of grief. I'm sure we're just trying to be sensitive and loving when we use expressions like, "she went to heaven." It's just that we're at a loss for the right words.

David Kessler, the master of all things related to grief, offers a better way. His website, Grief.com, shows how we can recognize loss and comfort those in mourning. I highly recommend it. [5]

When offering sincere condolences, we should consider how well we know the bereaved and our relationship with them, Kessler said. Are they a close friend? A coworker, teacher, or neighbor?

Here are three gentle condolences from Kessler's website. Please see his website (Grief.com) for more:

- I wish I had the right words; just know I care.
- My heart goes out to you during this painful time.
- I don't know how you feel, but I am here to help in any way I can.

ANECDOTE: LETTING MOM GRIEVE (CAREN'S STORY)

During the writing of this book my Mom's boyfriend died. Miraculously, Stan had lived to the age of ninety-two despite several life-threatening illnesses in his youth and old age. So his death wasn't unexpected.

But Mom's refusal to accept my support was. Mom and Stan had been together about fourteen years, and I was happy she'd found a companion. They truly enjoyed each other's company, at home and while traveling across the U.S. and Canada. But Stan's health had declined significantly in his last several years. He'd started to suffer from dementia, used a wheelchair full-time, and required a great deal of mom's assistance.

While Mom and I are similar in many ways, we're very different people. I'm much more sensitive. I wear my emotions on my sleeve. That goes for tears as well as joy, enthusiasm, and anger. Mom is more private, preferring to maintain composure and keep her tears to herself.

In fact, we'd clashed shortly after my father died two decades ago. Maybe I shouldn't have been surprised by Mom's reaction on the phone when I'd offered to be there for her. Here's how it went:

"Mom, I'm going to come down there to help you."

"No. Absolutely not."

"Well, then I'll call you back tomorrow."

"No."

"How about I call you in a few days?"

"No. Don't call me. I'll call you."

I felt rejected. I thought she'd appreciate my offer of comfort and support.

Growing up with my father's alcoholism and violent rage, I'd committed in my early thirties to mend my love-hate relationship with him and my miserable outlook on life. I've done an enormous amount of therapy and inner work on forgiveness, compassion, and releasing anger. I've also come to understand and respect my Mom, whom I'd once resented for staying with my father and allowing us to witness his abuse. Even when Dad's drinking wreaked havoc on his personality – transforming him from a lovable, intelligent, and charming man into an angry, brutal monster – mom had still loved him dearly.

Emotional and confused after the phone call, I started to write her a text: "Mom, please don't shut me out."

By the grace of God, I stopped myself and erased it. This wasn't about me. It was about her. This was her life, her relationship, and her time to grieve in her own way. I needed to honor that.

It was hard. At first, I thought of driving there anyway, despite her wishes. But I didn't. For nine days I refrained from calling her, although I did send a sympathy card and an email. Each morning, I'd wake up and think I'm going to call Mom today. Then I'd catch myself and back off.

Finally, I called her. From what I could tell, she'd been coping as well as could be expected. In fact, she didn't recall telling me no. She'd been exhausted from the week leading to Stan's death, going days without sleep. She'd been operating in control mode, a strength that had gotten her through months – if not years – of caring for Stan. She'd probably been in shock when she called me after his death.

As time passed, I asked myself what I'd learned from the experience. I think we all have different styles of expressing grief that are unique to who we are. This isn't the time to take things personally. At any given moment, we may be experiencing a different stage of grief than our family members. While one of us is approaching acceptance, the other may be overwhelmed by sadness. While one of us is in shock, the other may be angry.

As difficult as it may be – because we are mourning, too – we must give others the space and time to grieve in their own way.

QUESTIONS FOR REFLECTION

1. What is your position on the afterlife?

2. Have you struggled with what to say to someone who just lost a loved one?

3. Have you ever been on the receiving end of an awkward or inappropriate condolence? How did you react?

4. Have you heard a euphemism for death that wasn't on the list?

5. Have you ever felt "shut out" of mourning a loved one due to family conflicts? Was it ever resolved? If so, how?

SPARING LOVED ONES FROM A DIFFICULT BURDEN

"There is no greater gift you can give someone in grief than to ask them about their loved one, and then truly listen." — *David Kessler*

ONE OF THE most loving things we can do for our family is to plan ahead for our end-of-life care and death. This will go far to ease the burden on our spouse, partner, and children – a burden that may feel overwhelming when they're blinded by grief. If we're avoiding it, remember that we're doing it out of love for them. Think of it as a gift. It will go far to secure a legacy of caring and thoughtfulness.

This planning will include everything from an advance directive involving end-of-life wishes to burial or cremation, funeral or memorial service, and choosing someone to settle our finances and access our online accounts.

This is a huge part of our legacy, yet few people actually do it. About 92 percent of people say that talking about end-of-life care with their loved ones is important, but only 32 percent have actually done so, according The Conversation Project, an initiative which encourages end-of-life care wishes to be expressed and respected: [1]

> "Too many people are dying in a way they wouldn't choose, and too many of their loved ones are left feeling bereaved, guilty, and uncertain. It's time to transform our culture so we shift from not talking about dying to talking about it."

Dr. Ira Byock, a palliative care physician who founded the Institute for Human Caring in California, developed an advance care plan authorizing his wife to speak for him if he's incapacitated by a stroke, head injury, or some other catastrophic illness or injury.

Byock said he drafted the plan, "not to tie their hands, but simply to lift a bit of the weight of this burden from their shoulders." [2]

The remainder of this chapter provides valuable information and resources to help make critical end-of-life medical decisions and to plan for financial, personal, and legal issues. In addition, there's a comprehensive glossary (at the end of this book) to clear up confusing lingo.

LEGACY PLANNING

Gravestones have memorialized our ancestors for eons, but the digital age is transforming how we may remember our loved ones, said Suelin Chen, the co-founder of Cake, an online platform dedicated to planning death.

"We have a lot of millennials on our platform, and we see that this generation is very pragmatic and perceives less stigma about death than older generations," Chen said.[3] "I ask people, when your great-grandchildren search online for you in the future, what do you want them to find?"

Technological advances and entrepreneurial spirit have expanded the resources in this field. Companies, new and traditional, have made planning for the realities of life and death easier and more accessible:

Cake: Offers hundreds of articles on death, grief, mortality, and end-of-life preferences. It also has free personalized tools and a detailed checklist to help people understand what planning needs to be done before death.

Everplans: Helps with estate planning via an online organizational tool and an encrypted sharable vault to store all the personal, financial, health, and legal information loved ones will need.

FidSafe: Has an online tool to guide customers through the estate planning process, provides a checklist to organize critical documents, and offers secure online storage.

*While the authors list these companies as solid examples of the resources available, this is not meant to be an endorsement. Please do research and talk with family members and advisors before making decisions.

BY MAKING decisions ahead of time, we help our loved ones understand our personal values, life goals, and preferences regarding our future medical care.

End of Life Washington, an organization that works to raise the standard for end-of-life care, also offers a useful two-page worksheet with questions to consider before making decisions and preparing health care preferences.[4]

This planning doesn't always require a lawyer. Forms are available from the doctor, the local health department, and online. However, if there's a chance those directions will be challenged, it may be best to have a lawyer review it.

ADVANCE CARE PLANNING

This involves making medical preferences known to your doctor and family in case a serious injury or illness leaves you unable to make your own decisions. Sometimes the terms below are used interchangeably.

Living will: A legal document that describes the treatment you would want if you were to become terminally ill or permanently unconscious. For example, it would say whether you want ventilation, a feeding tube, palliative care to manage pain, or to donate your organs.

Durable power of attorney for health care: Identifies a person to make health care decisions for you if you were to become unconscious or unable to make medical decisions. It's also called medical power of attorney, or MPOA.

Physician orders for life-sustaining treatment (POLST): It's filled out by a doctor if you are diagnosed with a serious illness. It doesn't replace other advance directives but stays with you to ensure you get the medical treatment you want.

Do Not Resuscitate Order (DNR): A request for no cardiopulmonary resuscitation (CPR) if your heart or breathing stops. Best communicated by an advance directive form, it will be placed in your medical chart.

SETTLING YOUR FINANCES

Experts recommend that you develop a bills checklist – for bills on automatic payment and those paid manually – and keep it in a prominent place so a loved one can use it to change names on the account, cancel services, and shut down future billing.

BALANCE Financial Fitness Program offers a helpful checklist with a step-by-step action plan and a list of the documents and steps a surviving spouse, partner, or child will need. [5]

Use an accordion folder or waterproof container to keep these crucial documents:

- Will/trusts
- Life insurance policies
- Birth and marriage certificates
- Funeral arrangements
- Social security card
- Tax returns
- Divorce agreements
- Bank statements
- Stock certificates, investment account statements
- Pension/retirement plan statements
- Loan statements
- Mortgages, leases, deeds
- Motor vehicle titles, car insurance

- Homeowner's insurance
- Health insurance
- Safe deposit box information
- Storage locker contract and key
- Military service records
- Clubs or membership contracts

SOCIAL MEDIA PLANNING

Have you ever considered what will happen to your email and social media accounts after you die? Or, for that matter, your domain names, websites, blogs, digital rights to books, films, and other media?

Digital asset planning is the term for organizing these resources. It allows you to turn over your digital information to a designated person, known as a legacy contact, to handle these assets after your death.

DIGITAL ASSET PLANNING

- Consider getting a password manager, an online tool that securely manages login credentials.
- If this is unacceptable, put passwords, domain names, and other online access information on a single spreadsheet.
- A password alone may not be enough for your legacy contact to access your account. Provide all login information and the answers to security questions that were asked when the account was set up (such as place of birth, mother's maiden name, favorite movie, etc.).
- Keep photos and videos on a central backup site or on a hard drive.

Like many of us, you may have opened multiple social media accounts. If so, you'll need to address what you'd like to happen to your Facebook, LinkedIn, YouTube, and other social media accounts after you die.

Please note that these options were current at the time of this book's production and that media company policies change over time.

- As an account holder, you may choose to have your account permanently deleted.
- Many companies allow "memorialized accounts" for loved ones to share memories.
- Facebook and Instagram may permit a legacy contact to look after your account after showing proof of a death certificate or obituary.
- A friend or family member may create a separate group page so people can share memories of you.
- Google and YouTube generally work with family members or representatives to close an account to keep the information secure, safe, and private.
- Keep in mind that each social media company must be contacted individually because each has its own access rules.

ANECDOTE: HONORING OUR LOVED ONE'S WISHES

Several years before he died, Phillip had requested that he not be buried. He'd wanted his ashes scattered at sea because he had a special connection with the ocean and liked boating and swimming, even in the winter. We'd never have known this if he hadn't put his request in writing while making arrangements with the Neptune Society.

But Phillip was Jewish, and one rabbi told us he couldn't perform Phillip's memorial service without a burial due to Orthodox Jewish law. However, Rabbi Robert Goodman said he was fine with it if we buried Phillip's ashes in the cemetery. But Phillip had clearly stated he didn't want to be buried. So, this put me between a rock and a hard place. Eventually, the rabbis made an exception, saying that by being scattered at sea, Phillip's ashes were essentially going back to nature.

I gave Phillip's ashes to his daughter, a surfer who scattered them in the Atlantic Ocean off Jacksonville's coast.

I believe that in the first weeks after death, and even beyond that, our spirit knows how our body is being handled and memorialized. Spirit is aware of it and can see what's going on. I feel at peace knowing we'd reached an agreement that honored Phillip's wishes.

WRITING YOUR OBITUARY AND EPITAPH

"An awareness of one's mortality can lead you to wake up and live an authentic, meaningful life." — Bernie Siegel

AN OBITUARY IS A SHORT BIOGRAPHY, a tribute that's meant to notify the public that you have died. It emphasizes your life, not your death.

An obituary often includes funeral or memorial service details if they are available. Sometimes obituaries are causally referred to as a death notice. However, a death notice only contains the funeral or memorial service details.

In a best-case scenario, your obituary will run in your hometown newspaper and your local newspaper. But these days it's anybody's guess. For decades, newspapers have published obituaries as part of their commitment to public service. However, the news industry has changed dramatically in the last few decades. Many newspapers no longer publish obits due to reduced news staff and shrunken news sections.

Some newspapers that still publish obituaries charge a fee, others don't. Some large newspapers only publish obits for significant citizens. (Aren't we all significant?)

Over the last several years, news sources, funeral homes, and other companies have begun to provide online memorial pages. It's likely this will continue to be the platform for obits, unless a better solution comes along.

There are several reasons why it's better to write your own obituary: It will take the burden off your spouse, or other family member, who may be too upset to write it. It will make your obituary more historically accurate and comprehensive. And it will make you think about your own mortality.

That could be a good thing, said Megan Bruneau, a therapist and executive coach.

"What if, by ignoring our mortality, we're doing ourselves a giant disservice?" Bruneau asked.[1] "What if mindfully thinking about our own inevitable death – our finite existence, our impermanence – were healthy for living a good life?"

OBITUARY INFORMATION

Below is the type of information you should consider to craft a good obituary. Your obit doesn't have to include all these details, only those that are significant to your life.

Name: Official name and nickname

Date of birth

Place of birth

Favorite photograph

Reputation: Are you known for being witty or humorous? Generous? A good listener? Devoted friend? Hard worker, conscientious?

List family: Parents, spouse/partner, children, siblings, and grandchildren.

Love for spouse and family: How did you meet your spouse or partner? How did he or she change your life?

Education: Did you get a college degree or technical training? Only list high school or elementary school when it's significant.

Career: What industry do you work in? Do you own a business? Do you have professional achievements or awards? When did you retire?

Gifts and talents: Are you athletic, artistic, or intellectual? Have you won competitions or awards?

Military service: Have you served in the military? If so, what branch? What war? How long? Where? Rank? Commendations for bravery?

Military example: Gerald was a veteran of the Vietnam War, where he earned several medals, including the Purple Heart, Silver Star, and a Civil Action Unit Citation. He served three years with distinction as a U.S. Marine in Vietnam, including aiding in the evacuation and fall of Saigon. He was wounded during the evacuation of the U.S. Embassy and received other commendations for his dedication and bravery. The discipline and patriotism he learned in the Marines never left him.

Volunteering: Have you coached Little League Baseball or cheerleading? Volunteered at a hospital, fed the homeless or worked with Habitat for Humanity?

Hobbies: Are you a runner, gardener, weaver, skier, or hiker?

Faith, religion, spirituality: Do you belong to a church, synagogue, temple, or spiritual center? Have you served as an usher, prayer chaplain, or Sunday school teacher?

Wishes: Such as in lieu of flowers, please donate to a local food bank, hospice, church, or a charity of your choice.

OBITUARY WRITING TIPS

- You may find it hard to write about yourself, so don't be afraid to solicit insights from a spouse or friend on what to include or exclude.
- Limit details on cause of death. Some obituaries don't state how the person died – this is purely a personal decision.
- Keep length from roughly 250 to 350 words.
- Self-edit to ensure your details are correct. Double-check the spelling of people's names, places, and organizations.
- Ask several people to proofread your obit when it's finished.
- The person overseeing your funeral arrangements can add funeral or memorial service information to the end of your obit.
- Ask the funeral home to run your obituary in your hometown paper as well as your local paper (unless they are one and the same).

MY OBITUARY EXAMPLE

Mother, Author and Spiritual Intuitive Has Died

BETTY MAY "ALISA" Powell, a mother, caregiver, and intuitive who generously encouraged others, died (date to be added here).

Born May 5, 1942, in Joplin, Mo., Alisa was one of 11 siblings.

Known as a spiritual person, Alisa was always ready to share her time and talents and promote peace among people. She loved to make people laugh, even at her own expense, and had a gift for helping others see their true self. She always said that everyone's true nature is love, arising from the divine within.

Alisa married four times, twice to the same man. She fell for Robert and his positive, gentle nature at a church party in 2015. Married the following year, she truly admired his kindness, faith, and devotion to his family.

Alisa became a fan of lifelong learning. She was certified as a massage therapist, colon therapist, yoga instructor, aesthetician, and Reiki master. She also ran a cleaning business and took great satisfaction in beautifying people's homes.

Over the years, Alisa sang in two church choirs, taught Sunday school to young children, and volunteered to coordinate talent shows, luncheons, and other activities. More recently, she was a prayer chaplain at Unity Church for Creative Living in the St. Johns community, providing comfort and prayer for church members.

After retirement, Alisa co-authored a book, "Remember Me: How to Create a Spiritual Legacy of Love and Light," to help people find more meaning in their life and their death. She also took mediumship training to strengthen her intuitive and psychic abilities.

Alisa is survived by her spouse, Robert, and her daughters Kelly Conrow, of Gallatin Gateway, Mont., and Lisa Ross of Las Vegas; four grandchildren, Shane Estep, Jacob Estep, Jessie Contreras, and Alexis Conrow; and three siblings, Elizabeth Alexander, Margaret Lyster, and Gene Foley. She is predeceased by her son, Kevin Sean Conrow, and her grandson, Luke Z. Conrow.

HEADSTONE EPITAPH

Writing an epitaph is challenging because it needs to express what made the person special, all in one line. It must honor their life and be short enough to inscribe on their headstone.

Depending on the person's nature, an epitaph can be light-hearted, inspirational, or profound. Below are some examples: [2]

- "I had a lover's quarrel with the world." – Robert Frost
- "Free at last. Free at last. Thank God Almighty I'm Free At Last." – Martin Luther King, Jr.
- "I never met a man I didn't like." – Will Rogers
- "Well this was fun, let's do it again sometime." – Quniaron Bellthing

MY EPITAPH CAME from my obituary:

"Our true nature is love, arising from the divine within" – Betty May "Alisa" Powell

WRITING YOUR SPIRITUAL LEGACY

"As long as we live, they too will live; for they are now a part of us as we remember them." — Sylvan Kamens and Rabbi Jack Riemer

EVERYBODY HAS A STORY TO TELL. Your spiritual legacy is your story – how you've lived your life, and how your values, experiences, and choices have shaped who you are.

Much more personal than an obituary, your written spiritual legacy is only meant for your loved ones. The goal is to capture the essence of who you are: to convey your character, beliefs, life lessons, and your innate skills and talents.

Why write a spiritual legacy? Because sharing what you're made of and how you've met life's challenges can bring comfort, connection, and guidance to your loved ones down the road.

Writing this document may also help you see the big picture – maybe even your life's purpose. It will record how you've evolved, not despite the obstacles on your path but because of them. That life's hardships didn't happen to you *but for you,* by God's grace, to help you build endurance, wisdom, and a more fulfilling life.

Sometimes referred to as an ethical will, this legacy document is not legally binding: it will accompany your legal will.

Jews have embraced ethical wills for centuries to pass on deeply held values and beliefs. In the introduction to his book, "So That Your Values Live On," Rabbi Jack Riemer explains why we need to pursue life's universal questions:

"I have learned that ethical wills have the power to make people confront the ultimate choices that they must make in their lives. They can make people who are usually too preoccupied with earning a living stop and consider what they are living for." [1]

A good example is a brief legacy story on Professor Irving Goleman by his son, psychologist Daniel Goleman, the author of "Emotional Intelligence." The father, who died in 1961, left a lasting impression on many.

Daniel Goleman recalled his father's wholehearted commitment to his students at the University of the Pacific, noting he routinely woke at 4 a.m. to polish class lectures and customize assignments for each person in his class.

"He was an enormously dedicated teacher, and – I'm told by his former students – a riveting lecturer," Goleman said of his father. [2]

Those former students, who had attended a fiftieth class reunion, recalled professor Goleman's history and literature classes as the only courses that stuck with them after half a century. One of those students, jazz great Dave Brubeck, dedicated an oratorio, "Light in the Wilderness," to professor Goleman. [3]

While you'll be remembered in a uniquely different way, you can be certain that you, too, have had an impact on the world, or at least on your close circle.

VALUES GUIDE LIFE CHOICES

Have you ever considered how you'll be remembered? That's the crux of your legacy and it begs deep reflection. Maybe you'll be remembered for demonstrating love and loyalty to your family. Or how you mentored interns or new employees at the office. How you wore your heart on your sleeve. How you drove a cancer patient to and from treatment. How your baseball coaching helped build a child's confidence. Or the way you put people at ease, made them laugh, built them up, or worked behind the scenes to let other people shine.

As you begin to identify your personal traits and values, think of them collectively as an internal compass that's guided you through life. That's aligned your values with your life choices.

- Recall how you were as a young child, before you became self-conscious or worried about what other people thought of you. What interested you then?
- Consider how you've dealt with difficult events, relationships, or obstacles in your life? Has that changed over time?
- Think about how you have, or haven't, overcome certain fears, such as flying, public speaking, or using technology. If you did, what personal traits helped you? If you didn't, what held you back?
- Note whether you've ever had an epiphany, or a major shift in your perspective? If so, how did it change the course of your life?

TWO LISTS AND 12 QUESTIONS

To help you write your spiritual legacy, we've provided two lists to identify some of your personal characteristics. They won't capture the full picture of who you are, but they will provide a good starting point. These two lists are followed by a dozen questions that invite deep reflection or prayer.

Note: You may want to collaborate with a spouse, partner, or close friend on this project to help you identify "blind spots" that you don't see in yourself.

LIST 1: PERSONAL CHARACTERISTICS

Review the personal characteristics below and select 10 that resonate with you.

Idealistic

Broad-minded

Unconventional

Conscientious

Competent

Orderly

Dutiful

Ambitious

Self-disciplined

Deliberate

Sensitive

Generous

Spiritual

Warm

Funny

Understanding

Anxious

Angry

Depressed

Self-conscious

Impulsive

Perfectionist

Friendly

Assertive

Active

Positive

Adventurous

Agreeable

Trusting

Gentle

Compliant

Modest

Straightforward

Kindhearted

Peaceful

THE BRAVERY OF SELF-ASSESSMENT

While the traits on the previous pages mostly focus on positive characteristics, it's also important to recognize the not-so-positive parts of yourself that you might avoid – the habits that can be destructive and harm relationships. Sometimes these unflattering traits are referred to as our shadow. Perhaps you're already aware of them. Maybe someone has pointed them out to you.

Why is this an essential part of writing your spiritual legacy? Because these traits most certainly have contributed to your life lessons. Working on yourself takes patience, self-forgiveness, and effort over time: it's a lifelong process. This inner work shows self-awareness, the courage to be vulnerable, and a commitment to your personal and spiritual growth.

Taking stock in yourself may be difficult: You'll need to look at yourself objectively and honestly to discover things of which you may, or may not, be aware. Keep in mind that the traits on the next page are universal: everyone has some of them. They don't define who you are. This assessment will show how you may be taking responsibility for your own thoughts, attitudes, and behaviors. Please don't indulge in shaming or self-criticism during this review, but approach it with the same gentleness and compassion you would want others to show you.

LIST 2: PERSONAL DEEP DIVE

Choose 3 of the personal traits below. Do you see yourself in any of them? If so, have you made improvements?

Cruel: Inflicting pain or suffering on others because you can.

Deceitful: Purposely giving a false impression.

Dishonest: Being predisposed to lying, deceit. Not doing what you say.

Disloyal: Changing your allegiance whenever it suits you. Unreliable.

Greedy: Desiring more, regardless of how much you've already accumulated.

Immoral: Violating morale codes. The end justifies the means.

Impatient: Inability to wait your turn. Restless, quickly irritated, or provoked.

Judgmental: Rushing to harsh judgment about people, excessively critical.

Lazy: Unwilling to work or use energy. Idleness or care-lessness**.**

Narcissistic: Basking in ego, only believing good things about yourself.

Pessimistic: Always expecting the worst possible outcome. Bringing people down.

Petty: Acting with cruelty on matters little importance. Small-mindedness.

Prejudicial: Preconceived opinion without just grounds, disregarding a person's dignity and rights.

Selfish: Caring only for your own welfare above other people's.

Thoughtless: Disrespectful, not paying attention to the consequences for others.

Unforgiving: Holding onto anger and resentment toward someone else or yourself.

Untrustworthy: Consistently showing signs of being not dependable.

Vengeful: Seeking revenge by inflicting punishment for some prior offense.

HOW TO WRITE YOUR LEGACY

While writing is simply a way to organize your thoughts, the process isn't always simple. If you struggle with writing, you may find it easier to capture your thoughts with bullet points containing a single phrase or sentence.

This book is not only meant to help you write your spiritual legacy, but to help me write mine. So, you'll see an example of my personal review and legacy on the following pages.

SUGGESTIONS

- First, find quiet time to reflect on your personal characteristics you've chosen from the two lists. Consider how they've guided your life choices, your life's purpose, and how people may remember you.
- Write roughly 10-12 bullet points to show how these characteristics have shaped your life. This will help you develop a rough outline. Arrange them so they make sense, especially points that relate to each other.
- Then answer the 12 questions on the next page.
- Take your time with this process. Please approach it with patience, humbleness, and honesty. You can always come back later to expand or update it.

- Keep in mind that the people who will be reading this love you for who you are. They will find inspiration in your sincere self-appraisal.

12 QUESTIONS FOR CONTEMPLATION

- What are your gifts and abilities? (Identify about 5)
- How have your abilities guided your purpose in life?
- What is the purpose of your life?
- How have you overcome obstacles to achieving your goals?
- Who has influenced you the most and how? Who is your mentor, coach, or hero?
- Has your faith evolved over time? If you have had an epiphany, how did it affect your life?
- What is your position on the afterlife?
- What are your aspirations for your loved ones?
- Was (or is) there something you need to be forgiven for? How did you, or do you, plan to resolve it?
- Are you still holding a grudge against someone? Can you forgive them?
- If you knew you were going to die in six months, how might you live differently today?

ALISA'S PERSONAL CHARACTERISTICS

To be authentic and show how the process works, I'm sharing my own personal review and spiritual legacy. Here we go:

POSITIVE CHARACTERISTICS

- Unconventional
- Sensitive
- Understanding
- Friendly
- Funny
- Kindhearted
- Gentle
- Generous
- Perfectionist
- Spiritual

NEGATIVE TRAITS

- Impatient
- Judgmental
- Unforgiving

ALISA'S SPIRITUAL LEGACY

To my dearest family and friends,

- I want you all to know how much I love you and always have.
- I appreciate each of you for your individuality and uniqueness.
- I know some people in my family think I'm eccentric (unconventional). They're probably right and I'm OK with that.
- I'm proud of each of you, your accomplishments, and who you've become as a person.
- I regret that I haven't said this enough.
- We all know I wasn't a perfect mother, but I did the best I knew how at the time. I've acknowledged this and have learned to forgive myself.
- I've grown a lot since then, mentally, emotionally, and spiritually.
- I hope you can see that from our visits, phone calls, emails, and letters.
- I was always there for you when you needed me.

What are my gifts and abilities?

- I have compassion for people less fortunate than me.

- I'm a good listener who approaches people with an open heart.
- I'm generous with my time and donations to food banks, holiday toys, and other causes.
- I've been a prayer chaplain and have a passion for praying for others who are in need.
- I love helping people in need because I've been in their shoes and know how it feels.

How have my abilities and characteristics guided my purpose in life?

- My spiritual and intuitive nature has helped me sense other people's pain and feel a connection to them.
- My efforts to understand others have helped me be more thoughtful of the challenges they face.
- I have no fear of talking to people, hugging them, reminding them of their true nature, and trying to bring out the best in them.
- I know how to comfort people and put them at ease.

What is the purpose of my life?

- My soul's purpose is to know my true essence, which is God within me.

- To have my children
- To write this book
- To make sure every public bathroom has toilet paper, soap, and hand towels. (Go ahead. Laugh. Those closet to me know it's true!)

How have I overcome obstacles to achieving my goals?

- I've been wanting to write this book since 2013 but life got in the way.
- That includes my previous husband's illness and subsequent death in 2015.
- And my own heart attack in November of that year, which required stents and healing.
- Then Robert and I got together, got married and moved into the new house in 2016.
- Unsure how to start this book, I put it out to the Universe that I needed help. God's messengers, or angels, lead me to my co-author, Caren.
- Our writing process was interrupted by Covid-19, Robert's stroke and Caren's broken leg/ankle, which all occurred in 2020.
- At several points I grew impatient and was ready to give up on this book. But it was important to complete it because I have a history (it pains me to say) of not finishing projects. And I wanted to finish my spiritual legacy for my family.

Who has influenced me the most and how? My mentor, coach, or hero?

- Jesus is my guide, demonstrating love, compassion, and patience.
- He's shown me how to love, to see the truth of who I really am, and that I'm a soul in human form.
- I know I'm a kinder person because of Him.
- Jesus helped me learn to love myself, despite my shortcomings.
- I've learned that we all have our own crosses to bear, issues to face, and challenges to overcome.
- I've learned that I'm relieved of those burdens when I surrender myself to God.

Has my faith evolved over time? If I've experienced an epiphany, how did it impact my life?

- I've resisted many religions due to certain creeds and judgments that I can't embrace.
- As a result, I'm more spiritual than religious.
- I've developed a closer personal relationship with God and believe there are many truths and paths to God.
- I've learned that God's divinity, love, and light exist within me, not in a church. However, I do feel at home at the UCCL or the temple.

- The butterfly symbolizes my spiritual transformation over time and my connection with my deceased son, Kevin.

What is my position on the afterlife?

- I believe the soul is eternal and never dies.
- When we die, the ego and the physical body – the material aspects of life – come to an end. We embody our soul, our true essence that's the seat of God.

What are my aspirations for my loved ones?

- That they will discover the divinity and peace that lives within them.
- That they will learn to find happiness inside themselves, not in material things. Remember, it's just stuff.

Was (or is) there something I need to be forgiven for? How do I plan to resolve it?

- I spanked my daughter Kelly with a hairbrush when she was about five.
- I also spanked Lisa after her father and I came home drunk one night (no excuse, really).

- Both times, I reacted out of frustration and anger.
- Both times I regretted it immediately.
- I have apologized to each of them, but they said they don't remember it.
- I still remember it, and it hurts my heart. So, I've had to practice self-forgiveness.

Am I still holding a grudge against someone? Can I forgive them and let it go?

- I wrote my sister a letter about some hurtful childhood experiences and mean words between us.
- I felt that sending it to her would have caused more harm than good.
- I didn't mail it, but I got it off my chest by writing it down. I eventually threw it away.

If I knew I was going to die in six months, what would I do? How might I live differently today?

- I'd throw a big party, a farewell send-off with singing, dancing, food, and my favorite cake. I'd invite everyone to come say goodbye. No gloominess allowed!
- I don't think I would live differently.

As you finish your legacy, you'll want to write a closing message to instill a sense of hope and love for your loved ones. It can be thought-provoking, amusing, serious, or whatever tone you choose to take.

CONCLUSION

Everyone has a basic, universal need to be remembered. A need to know that our life has had meaning, that we strived to fulfill our purpose, and that our efforts didn't go unnoticed. I don't think any of us want to die without our loved ones truly knowing who we were.

We hope this book's personal stories and practical step-by-step guidance – as well as its action plan for end-of-life care and instructions for writing an obituary and spiritual legacy – will help readers achieve that goal.

Our spiritual legacy can be a blessing for ourselves and our loved ones. As we write it, we can review our life to see if we are living it the way we intended, and to change things if we aren't.

After we die, our legacy can offer a tangible way to share our aspirations for our loved ones and to help them stay connected to us. As an expression of our love, this legacy can also give them something to cherish and ease their sense of loss.

Our spiritual legacy is a personal story that confirms the endurance of the human spirit. It's a story that will be precious to our loved ones, their children, and for many generations to come.

GLOSSARY OF TERMS

Advanced care planning: The process of arranging late-stage healthcare plans, such as the type of medical care requested and who to trust in the case of an emergency.

Advance directive: The document that actually spells out a person's wishes for future medical treatment, (such as a living will) if the person is incapacitated and can't communicate it to a doctor.

Ashes: Also known as "cremated remains," the ashes are the material that remains after a body has been cremated.

Autopsy: An examination to discover the cause of death or the extent of disease when cause of death is unclear. Nearly all states seek an autopsy when someone dies in a suspicious, unusual, or unnatural way, including a suicide or if a public health threat is suspected.

Bequest for charitable donations (charitable bequest): Bequests are gifts made as part of a will or trust to a person, a nonprofit organization, trust or foundation. Anyone can make a bequest in any amount to an individual or charity.

Burial: Placing the body in a grave, usually a cemetery plot, following death. It often involves a casket and a headstone, although cremated ashes may also be buried.

Burial permit: A legal document used to authorize burial, cremation, or scattering of ashes. The funeral director usually obtains the burial permit on behalf of the family.

Celebration of life service: A casual, upbeat service to pay tribute to a loved one in a uniquely personal way, usually emphasizing the person's positive attributes.

Cremation: To reduce to ashes by burning. Some religious faiths, such as Islam, strictly forbid it. Cremation is usually cheaper than a burial and is followed by a memorial service, not a funeral.

Columbarium: A structure used to house urns with the cremated remains (ashes) of the deceased. It may be free-standing, or part of a chapel or mausoleum.

Committal service: The portion of a ceremony that involves speaking last words just prior to the burial.

Coroner (medical examiner): A public official whose investigates cause of death if it appears to be from other than natural causes, or if there was no physician in attendance for a long time prior to death.

Closed casket: A visitation where the casket is closed and the body is not available for viewing.

Death certificate: A legal document, signed by a medical professional or coroner, certifying the death of an individual.

Declaration of death: A death occurring at home, especially unexpectedly, requires an official declaration of death from a medical professional. The body will be taken to an emergency room for the declaration and then moved to a funeral home. Funeral planning can't start without it.

Digital asset plan: A plan to take care of financial records kept in smartphones, computers, or the cloud, to conduct financial transactions electronically, and to close email, social media accounts, websites, and other digital resources. The plan identifies a representative and provides all the information needed for them to access the accounts.

Digital executor: Someone who has been appointed to have access to digital assets or resources. Most, if not all, states have adopted Fiduciary Access to Digital Assets laws that govern this.

Disinter: To exhume, or remove from a burial site.

Do Not Resuscitate (DNR): A doctor's order that instructs health care providers not to do cardiopulmonary resuscitation (CPR) if a patient's breathing stops or the patient's heart stops beating. Wallet cards, bracelets, or documents are available to carry or have at home.

Durable power of attorney: An important estate planning tool that kicks into effect if a person become incapacitated, up until their death.

Embalming: A funeral practice that involves pumping formaldehyde into the deceased person's body to temporarily preserve it. It can help restore the dead person's appearance for a wake or open casket funeral.

Estate: The property and assets belonging to a person who has died, which may include real estate, money in bank accounts, shares, and personal possessions.

Ethical will: An ethical will is a document that outlines a person's values, life lessons learned, and hopes for the next generation. Rather than money or possessions, it aims to pass down values, beliefs, and ideals from one generation to the next.

Eulogy: A speech or piece of writing that praises someone highly, typically someone who has just died. May be given at a funeral or memorial service.

Executor: A person or institution appointed to carry out the terms of the deceased persons' will.

Fiduciary Access to Digital Assets Act: Law that governs access to a person's online accounts when they die or lose the ability to manage the accounts. Includes directions for the management of digital assets, such as computer files and website domains, and electronic communications such as email and social media accounts.

Funeral: A ceremony to honor a dead person. Usually, the body is present and the service is followed by a burial.

Green burial movement: Emphasizes natural decomposition of the body and environmental sustainability. It frowns on embalming fluids that contain formaldehyde, and cremation, which may generate airborne emissions.

Health care directives: Also known as a living will. See living will below.

Health care proxy (agent): Someone designated in advance to make health care decisions for a person who has become incapable of making their wishes known. The proxy has the same rights to request or refuse treatment that the incapacitated person would have had.

Hospice: Health care that focuses on making a terminally ill patient comfortable by addressing their pain and their emotional and spiritual needs. It's typically available when the patient has less than six months to live and wants to shift the focus from curative care to comfort care. Hospice care can be provided at home or in a center.

Interment: The act of placing a body in a grave or tomb, often following a funeral. Close family and friends may wish to be present to bid the deceased farewell.

Inurnment: The placement of cremated remains in an urn.

Legacy contact: A trusted family member or friend designated to oversee the dead person's Facebook (or other social media) account. They may manage it as a memorial page or close it down. They will be allowed to download the Facebook information for safekeeping.

Life-sustaining treatment (life support): Medical procedures that replace or support vital body functions, including CPR, breathing tubes, nutrition and hydration through tubes, and kidney dialysis.

Living will: Also known as a "health care directive," it contains the person's end-of-life wishes for doctors and family to follow. May include directions such as a do not resuscitate, and wishes regarding ventilation, a feeding tube, or pain management.

Mausoleum: A building that houses the casketed remains of a person above ground, instead of burial in a grave.

Medical Aid in Dying: When a terminally ill, mentally competent adult gets a prescription from a doctor that they can self-administer to achieve a peaceful death. It is legal in ten states in the U.S. and the District of Columbia.

Memorial service: A service to memorialize a deceased person when their body isn't present. It may be casual or traditional, simple or formal. It may occur in a place of worship, a funeral home or at someone's home.

Neptune Society: One of the largest cremation companies in the U.S. that offers prepaid plans and localized services across the country.

Obituary: A notice announcing a person's death in the newspapers or online. It may have biographical information about the deceased, surviving relatives, funeral arrangements, and other information requested by the family.

Officiant: A person who leads or officiates a funeral or memorial service.

Open casket: The casket is open for viewing; meant to provide solace to mourners by letting them see the deceased at peace.

Organ donation: The process of transplanting organs or tissues from one person into another. It begins with consent and registration, such as a notation on a driver's license. It will not interfere with medical care.

Ossuary: A container or room where the bones of dead people are placed.

Palliative care: A type of medicine offering compassionate and effective patient care for people with intractable pain at the end of life.

Personal representative: A person who has been appointed to manage and/or distribute the dead person's estate and to settle their financial affairs. Executors and administrators are both personal representatives.

Plot: A specific piece of ground in a cemetery that's owned by a family or an individual. It is used to bury a body in a casket or urn containing cremated remains.

Power of attorney (general): Gives the appointed person the right to sign documents, pay bills, and conduct financial transactions. A general power of attorney ends upon death or incapacitation.

Scattering: The act of distributing cremated remains (ashes) of the deceased as an act of remembrance.

Undertaker: Also known as the funeral director, this is the staff member who works with the family of the deceased to arrange the funeral, cremation, or other funeral services.

Urn: A container designed to hold the cremated remains or ashes of the deceased, either on a temporary or permanent basis.

Viewing: An informal gathering before the funeral for relatives and friends to pay their respects to the deceased and to share grief and support for one another. The body or a memorial to the deceased will likely be displayed. Also known as visitation or calling hours.

Wake (Vigil): A watch held beside the body of someone who has died. It may take place the night before the funeral and may last the entire night.

Will: A legal document that details how the deceased's estate (real estate and personal property) will be managed and distributed after death. Without a valid will, the person will have died intestate, which means the estate will be distributed according to the laws of the state in which the person resided.

REFERENCES

Please note that the websites below may change without notice

INTRODUCTION

1. "Carl Jung. Inner Authority," Fr. Richard Rohr, *Center for Action and Contemplation*, Nov. 21, 2021, https://cac.org/inner-authority-2021-11-21/

1. WHAT IS A SPIRITUAL LEGACY?

1. "Time Out of Time: Farewell to Madeleine L'Engle," *Books for Kids*, Sept. 10, 2007,

http://booksforkidsblog.blogspot.com/2007/09/time-out-of-time-farewell-to-madeleine.html

2. "Joan Halifax and Her Robe of Many Tears," Stephen Foehr, *Lion's Roar*, Nov. 1, 1997, https://www.lionsroar. com/joan-halifax-and-her-robe-of-many-tears/

3. "Hear My Voice: Patients Get a Chance to Put Their Legacy on Paper," Beba Tata, *National Association of Catholic Chaplains*, January/February 2019, https://www. nacc.org/vision/january-february-2019/hear-my-voice-patients-get-a-chance-to-put-their-legacy-on-paper/

4. Mendoza, Brishette, Diallo, Amadou, "The Best DNA Testing Kit," *The New York Times*, Dec. 10, 2021, https:// www.nytimes.com/wirecutter/reviews/best-dna-test/

5. "The Meaning and Meaninglessness of Genealogy: Researching our Family Background is All the Rage, But What does it All Mean?" Nathan H. Lents, Ph.D., *Psychology Today*, Jan. 29, 2018,

https://www.psychologytoday.com/us/blog/beastly-behav ior/201801/the-meaning-and-meaninglessness-genealogy

6. "Mementoes of Children's Lives Help Parents Through Grief," Jim Manzardo, *National Association of Catholic Chaplains*, January 2019,

https://www.nacc.org/vision/january-february-2019/memen toes-of-childrens-lives-help-parents-through-grief/

7. "Symbolic Immortality. Thoughts About the Future," Ernest Rosenbaum, MD; Eva Chittenden, MSW; Jane

Hawgood, MSW. *Stanford Center for Integrative Medicine* web page, Accessed April 22, 2022,

https://med.stanford.edu/survivingcancer/coping-with-cancer/symbolic-immortality-.html#:~:text=Our%20bio logic%20symbolic%20immortality%20legacy,our%20de scendants%20after%20we%20die.&text=The%20belief% 20in%20life%20after,most%20religions%20and%20spiri tual%20practices.&text=The%20afterlife%2C%20with% 20an%20immortal,involving%20death%2C%20rebirth% 20and%20resurrection.

8. Bible. 1 Kings 19:11-13. (English Standard Version)

2. COMMITTING TO FORGIVENESS

1. Mandela, Nelson. *Long Walk to Freedom: The Autobiography of Nelson Mandela.* Introduction by President Bill Clinton. Boston: Little, Brown and Company, 1994.

2. "Forgive, For Yourself if Not for Others: The Benefits of Forgiveness for All," Mark D. White Ph.D., *Psychology Today*, Dec. 23, 2010, https://www.psychologytoday.com/us/blog/maybe-its-just-me/201012/forgive-yourself-if-not-others

3. Patsy Cline, vocalist, "Side by Side," 1927, by Harry M. Woods (composer).

4. "The Hawaiian Secret of Forgiveness: Hoʻoponopono Can Help Anyone Let Go of Resentment," Matt James,

Ph.D., *Psychology Today*, May 23, 2011,

https://www.psychologytoday.com/us/blog/focus-forgive
ness/201105/the-hawaiian-secret-forgiveness

3. OUR TRUE ESSENCE IS GOD

1. Mandt, Elisabeth. *Intuitive Intelligence: Welcoming the Guest*." CreateSpace Independent Publishing Platform, 2011.

2. "The Natural Order of Things: A Sufi Master on Finding Balance in an Unstable World," Llewellyn Vaughan-Lee, *Parabola*, Balance, Fall 2020, https://parabola.org/2020/07/29/the-natural-order-of-things/

3. "Navigational Mechanisms of Migrating Monarch Butter-flies," Steven Reppert, Robert Gagear, Christine Merlin, *Trends in Neurosciences*, June 2, 2010, https://www.ncbi.nlm.nih.gov/pmc/articles/PMC2929297/

4. LOVE NEVER DIES

1. "Continuing Bonds: Shifting the Grief Paradigm," Litsa Williams, *What's Your Grief*, Feb. 17, 2014, https://whatsy ourgrief.com/continuing-bonds-shifting-the-grief-paradigm/

2. Rosenthal, Amy Krouse, "You May Want to Marry My Husband," *The New York Times*, March 3, 2017, https://www.nytimes.com/2017/03/03/style/modern-love-you-may-want-to-marry-my-husband.html

3. Rosenthal, Jason B., "My Wife Said You May Want to Marry Me," *The New York Times*, June 15, 2018, https://www.nytimes.com/2018/06/15/style/modern-love-my-wife-said-you-may-want-to-marry-me.html

4. "Later Life Marital Dissolution and Repartnership Status: A National Portrait," Susan Brown, I-Fen Lin, Anna M. Hammersmith, *The Journals of Gerontology*, September 2018,

https://academic.oup.com/psychsocgerontology/article/73/6/1032/2632068?login=true

5. GRIEF IS UNIVERSAL

1. "When Animals Grieve: Scientists are Uncovering Evidence that Humans Are Not the Only Animals That Mourn Their Dead," Barry Yeoman, *National Wildlife Federation,* 2018,

https://www.nwf.org/Home/Magazines/National-Wildlife/2018/Feb-Mar/Animals/When-Animals-Grieve

2. "A Message from David Kessler," *Grief.com* home page, Accessed April 12, 2022, https://grief.com/the-five-stages-of-grief/

3. Kessler, David. *Finding Meaning: The Sixth Stage of Grief.* New York: Scribner. 2019.

4. "In U.S., Decline of Christianity Continues at Rapid Pace. An Update on America's Changing Religious Landscape," *Pew Research Center*, Oct. 17, 2019,

https://www.pewforum.org/2019/10/17/in-u-s-decline-of-christianity-continues-at-rapid-pace/

5. "NFDA 2019 Cremation and Burial Report Reveals Fourth Consecutive Year of Growth for Cremation," *National Funeral Directors Association,* July 2019, https://nfda.org/news/media-center/nfda-news-releases/id/4395/cremation-is-here-to-stay-aging-baby-boomers-proved-cata lyst-in-shift-beyond-traditional-burial

6. FEAR OF DEATH AND HOW TO TALK ABOUT IT

1. "Languages of Grief: A Model for Understanding the Expressions of the Bereaved." Inge B. Corless, Rana Limbo, Regina S. Buosso, *Health Psychology and Behavioral Medicine*, Jan. 22, 2014, https://www.ncbi.nlm.nih.gov/pmc/articles/PMC4345827/

2. Ibid.

3. "Dying Is Absolutely Safe – Awareness Beyond Death," *Ram Dass Love Serve Remember Foundation*, Accessed April 12, 2022, https://www.ramdass.org/dying-is-abso lutely-safe/

4. Bush, Mirabai, and Ram Dass. *Walking Each Other Home: Conversations on Loving and Dying.* Louisville,

Colorado: Sounds True, 2018.

5. "The 10 Best and 10 Worst Things to Say to Someone in Grief," *Grief.com*, Accessed April 22, 2022, https://grief.com/10-best-worst-things-to-say-to-someone-in-grief/

7. SPARING LOVED ONES FROM A DIFFICULT BURDEN

1. "Most Americans 'Relieved' To Talk About End-of-life Care: New Survey by The Conversation Project Finds Cultural Shift Over Five Years," *The Conversation Project*, April 10, 2018, https://theconversationproject.org/wp-content/uploads/2018/07/Final-2018-Kelton-Findings-Press-Release.pdf

2. "Because I'm a Dad: Being a Loving Father Includes Planning for the Most Difficult Times in a Family's Life," Dr. Ira Byock, Sept. 5, 2019, https://irabyock.org/wp-content/uploads/2019/09/Byock-Because-I-am-a-Dad-Thrive-Global-Sept-5-2019.pdf

3. "Cake Will Sweeten the Process of Dying in the Digital Age" S. C. Stuart, *PC Magazine,* Jan. 6, 2019, https://www.pcmag.com/news/cake-will-sweeten-the-process-of-dying-in-the-digital-age

4. "Values Worksheet," *End of Life Washington*, Accessed April 22, 2022, https://endoflifewa.org/wp-content/uploads/2020/01/Values.Worksheet.fillable-01-10-2020.pdf

5. "Surviving Spouse Financial Checklist," *BALANCE Financial Fitness Program,* Accessed April 22, 2022, https://www.balancepro.net/education/pdf/survivingspouse.pdf

8. WRITING YOUR OBITUARY AND EPITAPH

1. "5 Reasons Thinking About Death Will Make Your Life Better," Megan Bruneau, *mindbodygreen*, Oct. 19, 2020,

https://www.mindbodygreen.com/0-14057/5-reasons-thinking-about-death-will-make-your-life-better.html

2. "Some Epitaphs of Famous People," Ralf Heckenbach, *Memorials.com,* June 2013,

https://www.memorials.com/blog/some-epitaphs-of-famous-people/

9. WRITING YOUR SPIRITUAL LEGACY

1. Riemer, Jack Rabbi. *So That Your Values Live On: Ethical Wills and How to Prepare Them.* Nashville: Jewish Lights Publishing, 1993.

2. "About Daniel Goleman," on Daniel Goleman's official website. Accessed April 22, 2022.

https://www.danielgoleman.info/biography/

3. Ibid.

ABOUT THE AUTHORS

Betty May "Alisa" Powell is a mother and intuitive who helps people find meaning in their life and their death.

Before she retired, she ran a home cleaning business. A life-long fan of learning, she became certified as a massage therapist, colon therapist, yoga instructor, aesthetician, and Reiki master.

She lives in Jacksonville, Fl with her husband Robert and their cat, Zen.

Caren Burmeister is a former journalist. After more than two decades, she left the newsroom in 2010. Now a free-lance writer and editor at Caren Tells Your Story, she helps others write inspiring stories that give meaning and purpose to life.

She lives in Jacksonville with her cats Brody and Gracie and enjoys yoga, photography, hanging out with friends, and hiking and whitewater river rafting in the Blue Ridge Mountains.